ON THE
BRIGHT
SIDE

FEELING GOOD WHEN THINGS SEEM BAD

ON THE BRIGHT SIDE

FEELING GOOD WHEN THINGS SEEM BAD

ED J. PINEGAR &
RICHARD J. ALLEN

Covenant Communications, Inc.

Published by Covenant Communications, Inc.
American Fork, Utah

Printed in The United States of America
First Printing: January 2010

16 15 14 13 12 11 10   10 9 8 7 6 5 4 3 2 1

ISBN-13: 978-1-59811-917-6

Contents

PREFACE

Heavenly Father and our Savior have as Their greatest desire that we can one day enter into a state of never-ending happiness (see Moses 1:39; Mosiah 2:41). Imagine being in a state of eternal happiness and rest—"which rest is a fulness of his glory" (D&C 84:24). In order to receive this great blessing, we must first go through a state of probation called mortality, wherein we face opposition and temptation and are tried and tested (see Abraham 3:25). However, from the words of Father Lehi in the Book of Mormon we learn this truth: the purpose of our mortality is that we "might have joy" (2 Nephi 2:25). This joy can begin right here and right now, and it can reach forward into the future, but there is a price to pay for happiness here and in the hereafter.

What must we believe and do to gain happiness—even in times of trial and tribulation? The counsel of Elder F. Enzio Busche begins to unfold the answer for us:

> Embrace this day with an enthusiastic welcome, no matter how it looks. The covenant with God to which you are true enables you to become enlightened by him, and nothing is impossible for you. . . . Put all frustrations, hurt feelings, and grumblings into the perspective of your eternal hope. Light will flow into your soul. . . . And finally, when you are compelled to give up something or when things that are dear to you are withdrawn from you, know that this is your lesson to be learned right now. But know also

that, as you are learning this lesson, God wants
to give you something better. (F. Enzio Busche,
BYU Speeches, May 14, 1996, 6–7)

In order to harvest feelings of peace and comfort, we first
strive to understand and apply the doctrines and principles
of the gospel to our lives. We live by the Spirit. We have a
desire to do good and be good, and, in facing life's trials and
disappointments, we remember the great truth taught by Lehi
about the nature of mortality and the role of opposition:

> For it must needs be, that there is an opposition
> in all things. If not so, . . . righteousness could
> not be brought to pass, neither wickedness,
> neither holiness nor misery, neither good
> nor bad. Wherefore, all things must needs be
> a compound in one; wherefore, if it should
> be one body it must needs remain as dead,
> having no life neither death, nor corruption
> nor incorruption, happiness nor misery, neither
> sense nor insensibility. (2 Nephi 2:11)

When we understand and appreciate the need for opposition
in all things, we have a better perception of the price we must
pay for happiness. Happiness does not just happen. Lasting joy
cannot be found in possessions, titles, stations, or anything of
this world. Fame and fortune are fleeting at best, while good
deeds of love and service last eternally. Unless our values are
centered in Christ and gospel truths, we will one day come to
realize that we are in the wrong place doing the wrong thing
and will thus never truly find joy and happiness.

Earth life is full of trials, tribulations, and temptations of
every variety. Such adversity is an integral part of the test of
mortality. The Lord said, "And we will prove them herewith, to
see if they will do all things whatsoever the Lord their God shall
command them" (Abraham 3:25).

The good news is that we have a way to feel good in spite of adversity. We have a way to see things clearly, to feel hope, to understand and appreciate those things that matter most. We have a way to find happiness. These blessings are all made possible through the Holy Spirit, which fills our souls with joy, love, peace, and comfort. We have been given doctrines and principles that teach us how to live "after the manner of happiness" (2 Nephi 5:27). The way is the gospel of Jesus Christ and the plan of salvation.

The purpose of this book is to remind us of the Lord's road map for feeling good—even when troubles and challenges seem overwhelming. As we start this journey, let us remember that we can have love, peace, joy, and happiness here on earth and can look forward to never-ending happiness in the world to come.

The Authors

PART ONE:
A JOURNEY TOWARD JOY

Lift up your head and be of good cheer.
—3 Nephi 1:13

"Men are, that they might have joy" (2 Nephi 2:25). So proclaims the oft-quoted scripture describing the purpose of our mortal existence. And yet life isn't always as enjoyable as we might wish it to be. Said President Thomas S. Monson, "Our journey into the future will not be a smooth highway stretching from here to eternity. Rather, there will be forks and turnings in the road, to say nothing of the unanticipated bumps" ("Treasure of Eternal Value," *Ensign*, Apr. 2008, 4). Nevertheless, with the right preparation, perspective, and attitude—and a few more tools—we can find joy in the here and now as well as in the eternities to come. "Brothers and sisters," President Monson said on another occasion, "my sincere prayer is that we may adapt to the changes in our lives, that we may realize what is most important, that we may . . . find joy in the journey ("Finding Joy in the Journey," *Ensign*, Nov. 2008, 87).

CHAPTER ONE
REST ASSURED, WE'RE ALL IN THIS TOGETHER

*Ye are . . . willing to bear one another's burdens, that
they may be light; Yea, and are willing to mourn with those that
mourn; yea, and comfort those that stand in need of comfort, and
to stand as witnesses of God at all times and in all things,
and in all places that ye may be in . . .*
—*Mosiah 18:8–9*

Among the few things we can be sure of in this life is the fact
that *everyone* will have problems and challenges. No one
can escape the trials and vicissitudes of life. Yet in our sojourn
here, we say and hear things like, "Why me?" "No one else has
the problems I have," and "This isn't fair." The reality is that
everyone faces problems and challenges—from the simple to
the catastrophic. This means *everyone.*

Dealing with Change. President Monson said on one
occasion:

> I begin by mentioning one of the most inevitable
> aspects of our lives here upon the earth, and that
> is *change.* At one time or another we've all heard
> some form of the familiar adage: 'Nothing is
> as constant as change.' Throughout our lives,
> we must deal with change. Some changes are
> welcome; some are not. There are changes in our
> lives which are sudden, such as the unexpected
> passing of a loved one, an unforeseen illness, the

loss of a possession we treasure. But most of the
changes take place subtly and slowly. ("Finding
Joy in the Journey," *Ensign,* Nov. 2008, 84)

Remembering the universality of adversity will give you
greater peace and understanding, confidence to deal with your
own struggles, and, above all, hope for a better tomorrow,
knowing and believing that sooner or later things are going to
be better.

To better understand your challenges from a broader
perspective, take a map of your community and put your finger
down on the place where you now live. Draw a circle around
that spot to encompass but a few blocks of nearby homes. At
any given time within that circle there are people experiencing
sufficient adversity for a lifetime of trials. Those who succumb
and let the light of courage flicker out lose twice—once to
the forces of misfortune and once to themselves as they let the
opportunity to rise above adversity slip from their grasp. Those
who muster the courage to fight on and overcome win twice—
once over the negative forces of circumstances and hardship
and once by taking control over inner attitude and personal
conviction—no matter what might happen.

Since we all face challenges, we can work together to buoy
each other up and help each other overcome. And when we
see it from an eternal perspective, adversity becomes the lens
through which we clearly see the joy of victory in doing the will
of the Father and eventually entering into his rest, "which rest is
the fulness of his glory" (D&C 84:24).

Prophetic Insights. Elder Joseph B. Wirthlin explained
how we can respond to adversity:

> The first thing we can do is learn to laugh. . . . The
> second thing we can do is seek for the eternal. . . .
> The third thing we can do is understand the
> principle of compensation. The Lord compensates

the faithful for every loss. That which is taken away from those who love the Lord will be added unto them in His own way. While it may not come at the time we desire, the faithful will know that every tear today will eventually be returned a hundredfold with tears of rejoicing and gratitude. . . .

The fourth thing we can do is put our trust in our Heavenly Father and His Son, Jesus Christ. ("Come What May, and Love It," *Ensign,* Nov. 2008, 26–28)

Blessings Await Us. An LDS author shared this experience about overcoming adversity:

> I was at a book signing and a sweet lady was sharing her travail over severe trials of every sort in life, including marital relationships that were coming to an end. She was sad and distraught. She was hurting. I signed a book for her and then visited with her for just a few moments. In those moments the Lord and the power of the Spirit performed a miracle and endowed her with hope. Promises were made on how the Spirit would comfort her and give blessings of happiness beyond her expectations. Years later, in a chance meeting, she related her happiness and the joy that the Lord in His goodness had given her through the blessings of the Holy Spirit.

As this story illustrates, truly the Lord and the Holy Spirit stand waiting to bless us with hope and the ability to overcome whatever difficulties arise. Blessings will always come to the righteous if they have the eyes to see and understand the things of the Lord. As we look at the traumatic happenings of life, we can recognize in each a magnificent lesson. We should pray for the courage to accept the trials of life, and at the same time, we can pray for specific blessings to be granted in accordance with God's will.

Peace After Tragedy. One good brother who lost a son in a tragic accident had this to say about accepting the Lord's will in facing life's trials:

> Our family faced a devastating trial when our son Cory was involved in a serious accident. We prayed and pleaded with Heavenly Father to spare Cory's life. We begged for a special blessing, but the answer was no. Our wonderful son went home to his Heavenly Father. We were heartbroken. But then during the funeral we received a special priesthood blessing of peace and comfort and felt a peace that transcends life itself. I cannot comprehend it, yet I accepted it and am eternally grateful for the power of the priesthood that a loving Heavenly Father gave to His children that they might be blessed through righteous priesthood leaders.

Remember, everyone has challenges, and we're all in this together. Whatever adversity we may face, we can endure it with support from those around us and help from on high. Joseph Smith, himself one of the greatest students of adversity in the history of the world, put it memorably in his inspired dedicatory prayer for the Kirtland Temple in 1836: "Help thy servants to say, with thy grace assisting them: Thy will be done, O Lord, and not ours" (D&C 109:44). And that is the key for finding joy in adversity. It is through the grace of God that the battle for joy and peace and harmony is ultimately won.

CHAPTER TWO
CHEERFULNESS: ATTITUDE DETERMINES ALTITUDE

A merry heart doeth good like a medicine.
—Proverbs 17:22

When it comes to dealing with any kind of challenge or problem, attitude makes an enormous amount of difference. Since problems and challenges seem to be an almost never-ending part of all of our lives, we must learn to deal with them. One of the simplest and most effective things we can do is make a habit of always looking on the bright side. As the proverbial truth has it, "A merry heart maketh a cheerful countenance: but by sorrow of the heart the spirit is broken" (Proverbs 15:13), and "A merry heart doeth good like a medicine: but a broken spirit drieth the bones" (Proverbs 17:22). Many people have related a story like this: "I was having just the lousiest day until Jan came by, and after visiting with her, I simply felt better. Her cheerful attitude and outlook on life lifted my soul. I am grateful for a cheerful and caring friend." Cheerfulness is one of the most uplifting and contagious attributes one can possess. It brightens both the giver as well as those who choose to receive it. It gives hope for the day ahead and even enhances physiological and emotional health. People can literally change in a few seconds when they encounter a cheerful person. Choose to be cheerful and change the world one person at a time. Especially yourself.

President Ezra Taft Benson advised: "Be cheerful in all that you do. Live joyfully. Live happily. Live enthusiastically, knowing that God does not dwell in gloom and melancholy but in light and love" (*God, Family, Country: Our Three Great Loyalties* [Salt Lake City: Deseret Book, 1974], 4). The Prophet Joseph Smith counseled, "Therefore, dearly beloved brethren, let us cheerfully do all things that lie in our power; and then may we stand still, with the utmost assurance, to see the salvation of God, and for his arm to be revealed" (D&C 123:17).

Attitude Is the Key. In the perpetually changing world around us, there are ups and downs every day, and in each situation our feelings and thoughts about our circumstances often determine our actions—and the ensuing results. We've all heard plenty of maxims on attitude and power: "Your attitude determines your altitude." "You are what you think you are." "When things get tough, the tough get going." "As a man thinketh in his heart, so is he." And the list goes on and on. A positive attitude is an important life tool that can help in all situations.

Prophetic Counsel. President James E. Faust said, "The Savior reminds us, 'All things are possible to him that believeth' (Mark 9:23), and 'All things shall work together for your good' (D&C 90:24). The attitude with which we submit to 'all things' is important. Maintaining a positive attitude and being cheerful are helpful. A belief that 'all these things shall give thee experience, and shall be for thy good' is like a spiritual stabilizer (D&C 122:7)" (*Reach Up for the Light* [Salt Lake City: Deseret Book, 1990], 83).

In the landmark discourse entitled "Come What May, and Love It," Elder Joseph B. Wirthlin teaches us some transcending truths about change and the way we face our challenges:

> How can we love days that are filled with sorrow? We can't—at least not in the moment. [In saying, "Come what may, and love it,"] I don't think my mother was suggesting that we suppress discouragement or deny the reality of

pain. I don't think she was suggesting that we smother unpleasant truths beneath a cloak of pretended happiness. But I do believe that the way we react to adversity can be a major factor in how happy and successful we can be in life.

If we approach adversities wisely, our hardest times can be times of greatest growth, which in turn can lead toward times of greatest happiness. (*Ensign*, Nov. 2008, 26)

Consider the following examples of people who chose to maintain a positive attitude even during great adversity:

- A ninety-seven-year-old woman who was blind and could barely hear said, "I am so grateful, for I can still go to the bathroom by myself and so many of my friends can't do that."
- A star high school athlete who had scholarships lined up for college contracted leukemia and never played ball in college. He recovered from the disease and bears the greatest testimony of the Atonement of Christ and how its power swallows up all our pain and sorrows. His dream was shattered, and yet his heart is full of gratitude and joy for the Lord and His goodness.
- A middle-aged man who faced a major financial crisis responded to his friend's sympathetic "I'm so sorry" by saying, "I'm not! I am so excited because I have come to realize how much I will be able to grow through dealing with this problem."
- A beloved mother began losing her eyesight. The vision in first one eye and then the other began deteriorating. Eventually, all she could see was a little light and shadows, though she could still read out of the corner of her eye. Her children gave her a device that magnified the printed page so she could read a few words at a time. Excitement filled the air as she explained the joy of being able to read again.

In all of these examples the main ingredient for happiness was the decision to face the situation with a cheerful attitude. Elder Carlos E. Asay admonishes us, "A positive mental attitude is really the result of faith and repentance. If a person has faith in himself or herself and God, he or she discards self-limiting thoughts, such as 'I can't do it.' If a person repents from past transgression, he or she pushes aside encumbering thoughts, such as 'I'm not worthy'" (*The Seven M's of Missionary Service: Proclaiming the Gospel as a Member or Full-time Missionary* [Salt Lake City: Bookcraft, 1996], 105). A positive attitude, along with faith that with the Lord's help we can overcome all things, is imperative in dealing with problems.

Be of Good Cheer. The Savior's repeated admonition about attitude in any situation is "be of good cheer." This phrase is used thirteen times in the holy scriptures. Here are some of the challenging situations we face in life and the reasons why we can truly "be of good cheer":

- **When you feel inadequate.** Read D&C 112:3–4, 10. Key point: *Forgiveness.*
- **When your faith is tested.** Read 3 Nephi 1:12–13. Key point: *The Lord fulfills His promises.*
- **When you feel poor and without resources.** Read D&C 78:17–22. Key point: *Spiritual wealth.*
- **When you feel weak or ill.** Read Matthew 9:2–8. Key point: *Healing.*
- **When you are fearful because of the elements.** Read Matthew 14:24–27; Mark 6:50. Key point: *The Savior is in charge.*
- **When you face danger on the Lord's errand.** Read Acts 27:22 and 25. Key point: *Safety in the Lord.*
- **When you face a daunting challenge.** Read Alma 17:31. Key point: *Follow the prophet.*
- **When you are called upon to bear testimony before the world.** Read D&C 68:3–6. Key point: *Inspiration.*

- **When you are persecuted for the sake of the gospel.** Read Acts 23:11. Key point: *Preservation until your mission is done.*
- **When you face evil.** Read D&C 61:36–37. Key point: *The Lord is with you.*
- **When you feel overcome with troubles.** Read John 16:33. Key point: Y*e might have peace; I have overcome the world.*

A good attitude is contagious and blesses not only you but also everyone with whom you associate. Remember, you can choose your attitude and your response in any situation you encounter. Choose to look at things in a positive way (e.g., the glass is always "half full" rather than "half empty"). Choose to be cheerful even when faced with adversity that seems insurmountable.

Positive attitudes bring blessings to your life in every respect. With patience, you can cultivate a positive attitude that will be enduring. From The Little Engine That Could to the athlete who picked himself up from sure defeat to go on to victory— experience proves time and again the power of a positive mental attitude. To cope with life, it is well not just to understand the value of a positive attitude, but to practice it as well. Decide now to move forward with a positive attitude and a cheerful heart.

Chapter Three
The Positive Role of Adversity

Know thou, my son, that all these things shall give thee experience, and shall be for thy good.
—D&C 122:7

Adversity is the reality of life. It can come from disease, accidents, physical or emotional injury, natural disasters, wars, or even ignorance. It can result from willful disobedience, but it can just as easily afflict an innocent victim (see Helaman 3:34). It can come as chastisement from the Lord or as a special trial He gives us for our particular tutoring and growth. It is always present, and if we can come to terms with it, we can learn to navigate the mortal pathways leading to a higher quality of life.

Of primary importance in coming to terms with adversity is realizing that opposition in all things is essential for our growth. Without opposition, we could not understand or appreciate joy in contrast to sorrow or righteousness in contrast to wickedness. Without opposition, everything would be "a compound in one" (see 2 Nephi 2:11)—devoid of vitality and bereft of the opportunity for eternal progression.

Opposition in all things is an eternal verity. It is necessary in order for us to grow. When we realize that adversity, trials, tribulations, and opposition are for our growth, then our attitude and behavior will change. Adversity will become an opportunity rather than a stumbling block. We need to look at life as the time to prove ourselves worthy—not just as a time to try to free ourselves of adversity.

In all the difficulties of life, let us never lose sight of our purpose. We are here to become like our Heavenly Father and our Savior Jesus Christ. We agreed to the test of mortality in the premortal life. We need this experience in order to grow. In our trials we learn how to help others by applying the lessons we learn, even as Christ did in suffering the ultimate sacrifice (see Alma 7:11–12; see also D&C 122:7; Mosiah 3:19). The Lord said, "My people must be tried in all things, that they may be prepared to receive the glory that I have for them, even the glory of Zion; and he that will not bear chastisement is not worthy of my kingdom" (D&C 136:31).

Heavenly Father knows what is best for us (see Proverbs 3:5–6). We become perfected through the process of sacrifice, enduring to the end, and learning to submit to all things that the Father sees fit to inflict upon us (see Mosiah 3:19). We can learn to cultivate an attitude full of hope and faith and go forward knowing of the goodness of God. As we come to understand and appreciate the doctrine of opposition, we will be filled with gratitude for the blessings and opportunities of life, and thus our attitude and behavior will change. We will indeed start to feel good, even when things seem bad.

Prophetic Counsel. President David O. McKay taught a magnificent truth when he said, "There are those who have met disaster, which almost seems defeat, who have become somewhat soured in their natures, but if they stop to think, even the adversity which has come to them may prove a means of spiritual uplift. Adversity itself may lead toward and not away from God and spiritual enlightenment; and privation may prove a source of strength if we can but keep a sweetness of mind and spirit" (Conference Report, Oct. 1936, 103; *Gospel Ideals: Selections from the Discourses of David O. McKay*).

This great truth is exemplified in the Book of Mormon. After experiencing the same trying event, some people changed for the better and some people changed for the worse. We read in Alma 62:41: "But behold, because of the exceedingly great length of the war between the Nephites and the Lamanites many had become hardened, because of the exceedingly great length of the war; and many were softened because of their afflictions, insomuch that they did humble themselves before God, even in the depth of humility." The same war caused two opposite reactions: some people became hardened and some became softened. We can always choose humility and submission to the Lord. We can allow adversity to draw us closer to the Lord when we truly believe that He wants the very best for us. When we sincerely seek His will over our own, we are showing Him our love in the only way we really can, because the only real gift we can give to our Heavenly Father is *our* will to accept *His* will—"Thy will be done." Can there be any greater joy and feeling of closeness to the Lord than when we cheerfully and willingly turn our will over to the Lord and lean not to our own understanding? Then we can, like Nephi, say:

> O Lord, wilt thou encircle me around in the robe of thy righteousness! O Lord, wilt thou make a way for mine escape before mine enemies! Wilt thou make my path straight before me! Wilt thou not place a stumbling block in my way—but that thou wouldst clear my way before me, and hedge not up my way, but the ways of mine enemy.
>
> O Lord, I have trusted in thee, and I will trust in thee forever. I will not put my trust in the arm of flesh; for I know that cursed is he that putteth his trust in the arm of flesh. Yea, cursed is he that putteth his trust in man or maketh flesh his arm. (2 Nephi 4:33–34)

We can all trust that the Lord will not give us more adversity than we can bear and that He will consecrate our afflictions for our good (see 2 Nephi 2:2). Then we can praise God even during our trials. Nephi, for example, was plagued by adversity and opposition at every turn—in obtaining the plates, building the ship, crossing the great ocean, and finally setting up the colony in the promised land—yet he praised the Lord and gave thanks (see 1 Nephi 18:16; 2 Nephi 4:30; 31:13). As President Ezra Taft Benson admonished us, "Our great purpose in life is to overcome adversity and worldly consideration as we strive for things of the Spirit" (*The Teachings of Ezra Taft Benson* [Salt Lake City: Bookcraft, 1988], 449–50). President Gordon B. Hinckley reminded us: "If as a people we will build and sustain one another, the Lord will bless us with the strength to weather every storm and continue to move forward through every adversity" ("Five Million Members—A Milestone and Not a Summit," *Ensign,* May 1982, 46).

In these afflictions and tribulations we have a source of relief: we can always remember to call upon the Lord in mighty prayer. The Prophet Zenos taught this plainly. He said, addressing the Lord, "And thou didst hear me because of mine afflictions and my sincerity; and it is because of thy Son that thou hast been thus merciful unto me, therefore I will cry unto thee in all mine afflictions, for in thee is my joy; for thou hast turned thy judgments away from me, because of thy Son" (Alma 33:11). Nephi of old and all the Saints both past and present received their strength and support from calling upon God in prayer in the name of His beloved Son, Jesus Christ. We can do so as well, with courage and valor.

Through prayer we will be strengthened and comforted. Each of us can and will be inspired, enabling us to grow through our tests here on earth and not succumb to tests and trials. Remember, adversity is a necessary part of the test of mortality, and the blessings for passing the test include greater joy than we can even imagine. When we commit to relying on the Lord rather than on the arm of flesh, we can overcome any trial and affliction. The question is, how can we gain a better perspective on adversity and learn to appreciate its role in our lives so that we can grow from our experiences? The following ideas may help you view and respond to adversity in a positive manner:

- **Adversity Is a Necessary Part of Life.** From the very beginning, adversity has been part of God's plan for the learning and growth of His children. We have already discussed the doctrine taught by Lehi that there must be opposition in all things in order for righteousness and good to exist (see 2 Nephi 2:11). Adam and Eve understood this, and thereby they were able to rejoice in the affliction of being expelled from the paradisiacal Garden of Eden and commanded to labor and toil in mortality. Indeed, adversity can lead to good, for learning to overcome adversity is part of life (see D&C 98:1–3). Adversity teaches us to trust in the Lord (see Proverbs 3:5–6). He chastens those He loves (see 2 Nephi 5:25; Mosiah 23:21) and then blesses those who triumph over adversity (see Mosiah 24:8–15).
- **We Have Access to Effective Tools for Overcoming Adversity.** In consigning His children to lives of opposition and adversity, our Heavenly Father did not leave us without the means of overcoming every challenge we might face. What tools do we have? We have faith in Jesus Christ, enabling us to receive the strength to overcome our adversity (see 1 Nephi 7:17). We have the word of God, empowering us to do all things that we should do (see 2 Nephi 32:3). We have the Spirit, guiding us in all aspects of our lives (see 2 Nephi 32:5) and comforting us in our challenges (see John 14:16). We have prayer—the divine channel for asking and receiving help from the Lord (see James 1:5–6; Mosiah 27:14; Alma 13:28). Moreover, we have hope, knowing that in the end all things shall work together for our good as we endure and transcend adversity (see D&C 122:7). Furthermore, we have patience because of the knowledge that time will become our ally as we respond in righteousness to adversity (see Alma 26:27). The process of overcoming was never meant to be easy or a quick fix but rather a process of becoming (see D&C 24:8). Additionally, we have the support of the people around us—family, friends, associates, and even caring strangers—who are also

undergoing the test of mortality. We can strengthen and lift each other (see D&C 108:7).

- **Great Benefits Come through Adversity.** In dealing with adversity, we should remember that not all of its effects are negative. If we allow it, adversity can bring us great benefits. Think of humility, for example. Humility, or being confirmed in our dependence upon God, serves as the beginning virtue of exaltation. Think of the self-worth and self-confidence generated when we overcome adversity. Think of the strength that comes when our victory over adversity brings us an enduring kind of spiritual vitality. Think of gratitude—adversity can be the teacher that helps us remember the good times and the blessings of God. Think of spirituality—the gift that comes when, through the challenges of life, we grow closer to God, knowing that He not only gives us the strength to overcome but also provides magnificent blessings in the process. And those blessings from the Lord witness unto us that the Savior continually nurtures us and strengthens us in our adversity and afflictions (see Alma 7:11–12).

In all of this, we can learn to deal with things that seem to be out of our control. We can rely upon the Lord (see 1 Nephi 3:7; Proverbs 3:5–6). We can seek counsel from our leaders and trusted friends (see Mosiah 18:8–9). We can ask for priesthood blessings. We can learn to forgive, for in forgiving, the healing process is made possible. Remember that healing is from the Lord, who succors and blesses us through the Atonement (see Alma 7:11–12). Things beyond our control are covered by the infinite and eternal Atonement of the Lord and Savior Jesus Christ. None of us should ever blame ourselves in such circumstances, but rather go forward in faith. Through faith all things can be done (see Moroni 7:33; 10:23).

Portraits in Overcoming Adversity. The lessons of history serve to remind us that people of courage and determination have found success and become notable influences for good in spite of what could have been debilitating difficulties. The following quote originally came from Ted Engstrom, but various authors have added to and modified it so it reads thus:

Cripple him, and you have a Sir Walter Scott. Lock him in a prison cell, and you have a John Bunyan. Bury him in the snows of Valley Forge, and you have a George Washington. Land him in poverty, and you have an Abraham Lincoln. Subject him to bitter religious strife, and you have a Disraeli. Strike him with Infantile Paralysis, and you have a Franklin D. Roosevelt, the only President of the United States to be elected to four terms of office. Burn him so severely in a schoolhouse fire that the doctors say he will never walk, and you have a Glenn Cunningham, who set a world record in 1934 for running the mile in 4 minutes 6.7 seconds.

Deafen a genius composer who continues to compose some of the world's most beautiful music, and you have a Beethoven. Drag him more dead than alive out of a rice paddy in Vietnam, and you have a Rocky Bleier, that beautiful runningback for the Pittsburgh Steelers. Have him or her born black in a society filled with racial discrimination, and you have a Booker T. Washington, Harriet Tubman, or Martin Luther King Jr. Have him born of parents who survived a Nazi concentration camp, paralyze him from the waist down at the age of four, and you have an Itzhak Perlman, the incomparable violinist. Call him "retarded" and write him off as "uneducatable," and you have an Albert Einstein.

After losing both his legs in an airplane crash, let an RAF fighter pilot fly, and you have World War II ace Douglas Bader, who was captured by the Germans three times and escaped three times on two artificial limbs. Label him too stupid to learn, and you have a Thomas Edison. Label him a hopeless alcoholic, and you have a Bill Wilson, the founder of Alcoholics Anonymous. Tell her she is too old to start painting at 80, and you have a Grandma Moses. Blind him at age 44, and you have a John Milton, who 10 years later wrote *Paradise Lost*. Call him dull and hopeless and flunk him in the 6th grade, and you have a Winston Churchill.

Tell a young boy who loved to draw and sketch that he had no talent, and you have a Walt Disney. Rate him mediocre in chemistry, and you have a Louis Pasteur. Take a crippled child whose only home was an orphanage, and you have a James E. West, who became the first chief executive of the Boy Scouts of America. Spit on him, humiliate him, betray his trust, say one thing and do another. Mistrust those whom he loves. Mock him. Make him carry a heavy wooden cross, and then crucify him, and you have the Savior of the world—and he forgives you and calls you a friend.

Adversity forges the greatest of men and women. And like these people, by serving others, we can forget our problems and enhance our capacity to cope with adversity. Remember that adversity and opposition are to temper us, not consume us, for in adversity, time is a great healer. And lest we forget, the only difference between stumbling blocks and stepping stones is the way you use them. There is hope as described by Napoleon Hill: "Every adversity, envy, failure, every heartache comes with the seed of an equal or greater benefit" (Patric Chan, *Success Quotes: Your Ultimate Inspirational Guide;* http://ebookdirectory.com).

Prophetic Counsel. Elder Jeffrey R. Holland said:

> I ask everyone within the sound of my voice to take heart, be filled with faith, and remember the Lord has said He 'would fight [*our*] battles, [our] children's battles, and [the battles of our] children's children.' [D&C 98:37] And what do we do to merit such a defense? We are to 'search diligently, pray always, and be believing[. Then] all things shall work together for [our] good, if [we] walk uprightly and remember the covenant wherewith [we] have covenanted.' [D&C 90:24] The latter days are *not* a time to fear and tremble. They *are* a time to be believing and remember our covenants. ("The Ministry of Angels," *Ensign*, Nov. 2008, 30)

We came to this earth to be tested to see if we would obey (see Abraham 3:25). In this test, opposition is the environment in which we can grow. With faith and commitment we can gain the wisdom to understand and appreciate, even as the Prophet Joseph, that all of this opposition will give us experience and will be for our good, for our growth in becoming like our Savior Jesus Christ (see D&C 122:7). When we recognize this, we can cope with adversity and opposition. The Lord will not give us anything that we cannot eventually overcome, for He strengthens us and will provide a way (see Alma 26:11–12; Ether 12:27; 1 Nephi 3:7). Through coming to understand the positive role of adversity in our lives, we can feel good, even when things seem bad.

CHAPTER FOUR
PERCEPTION: THE VIEW'S BETTER FROM UP HERE

Hereby perceive we the love of God, because
he laid down his life for us . . .
—1 John 3:16

All too readily your perception of life becomes your reality of life. Your perception is your understanding of things as they appear to you. Primarily, three things govern perception: past and present realities, value systems, and attitude. If there have been dominating negative experiences in your past, a distorted value system, or bad attitudes in your life, you may not see life as it really is. Your perception, the lens of your internal view of things, shaped by your unique framework of perception, could be subject to distortions. George Bernard Shaw reminds us: "Better keep yourself clean and bright; you are the window through which you must see the world."

Past and Present Realities. To see clearly requires that we deal objectively with past and present realities as an integrated whole. In that way, our view of the future will be more dispassionate and more principle centered. "As much of heaven is visible as we have eyes to see," according to a quote attributed to Ralph Waldo Emerson. If we abide by a value system based on true principles, we will cultivate a wholesome and winning attitude. To have a perfectly realistic perception of life—cherishing its deeper meaning and purpose—we need to understand the plan of happiness and our divine nature from premortal times, cultivate a value system anchored in the gospel of Jesus Christ, look at life with an eye of faith and hope centered on the Atonement, and thus have a positive, life-shaping attitude that will carry us forward toward our ultimate goal of immortality and eternal life. And as the Apostle Paul reminded us, even the most advanced of spiritual perception can hardly fathom the marvelous blessings that are in store for the valiant and obedient: "But as it is written, Eye hath not seen, nor ear heard, neither have entered into the heart of man, the things which God hath prepared for them that love him. But God hath revealed them unto us by his Spirit: for the Spirit searcheth all things, yea, the deep things of God" (1 Corinthians 2:9–10).

Understanding the past, present, and future brings a true perception. Understanding your past includes recognizing that you are a divine being having a variety of mortal experiences that constitute an environment of learning, personal development, repentance, and becoming. When you understand your past in this context—as an opportunity to pass the milestones of progress and do better each and every day—your perception improves. To understand your present, you must know that you are a being with agency, the God-given power to make defining and governing choices in life that will determine—beginning in the present moment—how you feel and how you unfold toward your divine potential. Understanding your future involves perceiving yourself as having the miraculous potential to fulfill the commandment of the Savior: "Therefore I would that ye should be perfect even as I, or your Father who is in heaven is perfect" (3 Nephi 12:48). This kind of authentic past, present, and future self-perception will open the way to wonderful experiences and relationships in your life.

Value Systems. Your values determine your direction and your perception. You can be principle centered by governing your vision in alignment with true principles. For example, if you perceive the world around you with overweening distrust and suspicion, remember the principle, "He who does not trust enough, will not be trusted" (Lao Tzu). If you feel that people are always against you, remember the principle, "Therefore all things whatsoever ye would that men should do to you, do ye even so to them" (Matthew 7:12). Set your priorities in order by creating and following a value system that is gospel centered, moral, and civil—one that elevates the people you care about to the top level of priority in your life.

Attitude. Likewise, your attitude will determine your perception. Your attitude is a precursor to everything you say and do—your responses and your actions, your learning and your relationships. Attitude is a fundamental, determining factor. The key is that, as we discussed in chapter two, your attitude is your own choice. You can elect to frame your experiences within a positive philosophy. By thinking with a hopeful view toward the future, you can maintain a positive disposition, thus allowing yourself to perceive opportunities beyond adversity, possibilities beyond tribulation, and blessings beyond the trials of life. Moreover, you can choose to be humble. A humble attitude encourages you to be easily entreated (see Alma 7:23), thus open to knowledge and counsel. Seek feedback from people you trust and admire. Ask simply, "Am I seeing this correctly?" and then listen carefully to their responses. You can search the scriptures and study the words of our living prophets. You can become informed about important issues by reading books, journals, and magazines. You can surf the Web for wholesome and instructive programming. You can thoughtfully study the issues before developing your own opinions. Above all, seek higher truth pertaining to your own course and direction in life. Pray and meditate. Be open to the whisperings of the Spirit.

A positive attitude can change everything. You can be what you want to be. Be realistically optimistic by choosing to guide your thoughts toward desirable outcomes. Be hopeful by believing with conviction that sooner or later things will be better. Forgive and look to the future, for, as Desmond Tutu counseled, "Without forgiveness, there is no future." You can accentuate your good points by focusing less on your perceived weaknesses and more on your strengths: "It is not what you are that is holding you back—it is what you think you are not," declares management expert Robin S. Sharma (*Timeless Wisdom,* http://www.scribd.com/doc/1938171/Timeless-Wisdom-Robin-Sharma, 2003, 31). Use positive self-talk by remembering that you have the power within you to make a difference. Proactively seek for the good by consciously going about the day with the intent of finding the positive. By looking for the good in everything, you will find a great deal more of it than you thought possible. You can change your environment by choosing to be around positive people, by cultivating a diet of uplifting reading material, by spending more time in nature in order to feel more alive and in tune with vital forces, and by seeking to live in an environment of light and truth. Also, work on your goals by getting out and doing meaningful things to support your objectives, thus bringing your perception into focus very quickly. Truly, with a positive attitude you can see things more clearly. You are free to see and do and become.

The Highest Perspective. In all of this you are wise to place things in the highest perspective—to look at things the way the Lord sees them. A true perception of life involves seeing things in the light of the gospel, which provides you with a value system, teaches you of your past and present realities, and changes your attitude through the power of hope. Many people find no joy in life because of their misperceptions, but those who view life through the lens of the gospel of Jesus Christ tend to be happier and to perceive life as an opportunity for joy and fulfillment. They understand that perception clarified through faith is vision. All of us need a vision of who we really are—sons and daughters of God with a glorious destiny. Take the time to be sure you see things clearly, with a spiritual vision. Be slow to judge, and aspire to accentuate the positive. Remember that life was made to be enjoyed.

CHAPTER FIVE
AGENCY: A CHOICE BLESSING

*Verily I say, men should be anxiously engaged in
a good cause, and do many things of their own free will, and
bring to pass much righteousness; For the power is in them, wherein
they are agents unto themselves. And inasmuch as men
do good they shall in nowise lose their reward.*
—D&C 58:27–28

Agency is a gift. The right to choose is an eternal verity. It is necessary for our growth. We are a result of the use of our agency. Our choices and decisions determine our blessings or the consequences of our actions. Agency can operate because there are (1) laws and commandments given by God, (2) knowledge of good and evil, and (3) opposition in all things. The freedom to choose is really moral agency, which connotes responsibility and accountability in regard to our choices (see D&C 101:78).

You have 86,400 seconds in each day to use as you choose. You are in control of your life. You can choose to accept or reject every situation. You can choose to obey the law or disobey the law. You can choose to use correct principles or go the way of the world. You can choose to set goals and make plans for success or do nothing. As Lehi explains, you "are free to choose liberty and eternal life, through the great Mediator of all men, or to choose captivity and death, according to the captivity and power of the devil; for he seeketh that all men might be miserable like unto himself" (2 Nephi 2:27). Every decision or lack thereof is a choice you make. These decisions will determine your destiny. This accountability is part of moral agency.

Moral agency connotes that we are accountable for our actions. We will be judged according to our actions. Christ is our judge and is the keeper of the gate (see 2 Nephi 9:41). We should have a great desire to keep His commandments because after this life, we will be required to look into His face, knowing that He paid the price for our sins. Alma felt the weight of this knowledge when he felt godly sorrow for his misdeeds. "Oh . . . that I could be banished and become extinct," he exclaimed, "that I might not be brought to stand in the presence of my God" (Alma 36:15). Later, using his agency to repent replaced his feelings of guilt and sorrow with indescribable joy: "I could remember my pains no more; yea, I was harrowed up by the memory of my sins no more. And oh, what joy, and what marvelous light I did behold; yea, my soul was filled with joy as exceeding as was my pain! Yea, I say unto you . . . that there could be nothing so exquisite and so bitter as were my pains. Yea, and again I say unto you . . . that on the other hand, there can be nothing so exquisite and sweet as was my joy" (Alma 36:19–21).

Since agency is such a choice blessing, we need to make sure we treat it as such. Some poor uses of agency result in consequences that limit our future use of this gift. Addictions enslave us and can lessen our ability to achieve wholesome and productive outcomes. Unwise financial decisions can shackle us with debt and lead to feelings of hopelessness, exacerbated through the incorrect perception that we are powerless to gain liberty through corrective procedures. And sin separates us from God, causing us to lose the Spirit and feel helpless and alone (see Mosiah 10:11–12; Alma 37:9). Worse still, sometimes we make the mistake of incurring the attitude that we can sin a little and receive a little punishment and then go on with life (see 2 Nephi 28:8). On the other hand, if we use our agency to stay free of addictions, govern our financial affairs wisely, and honor our gospel covenants with valor and faith, these choices will sharpen our capability to use our moral agency with exactness in following the will of the Lord. As a result, hope flourishes and happiness ensues.

You can use your agency wisely by using the light of Christ (Moroni 7:15–17) and living by the Spirit (2 Nephi 32:5). You have the power to make good decisions. Remember that when you fail to act when choices are placed before you, you are still using your agency by your decision to be passive or indecisive. Agency has two dimensions: the action of commission or the nonaction of omission. Passivity in the face of choice is agency by omission (failure to choose). In order to enjoy the full blessings of the gift of agency, we need to be conscious of both of these dimensions so that we can consistently exercise our agency in righteous ways.

The Relationship Between Happiness and Obedience. The laws of God are designed to bring us happiness. Obedience to the commandments in an environment of opposition and moral choice leads to joy—as the Savior said, "If ye know these things, happy are ye if ye do them" (John 13:17). The commandments are instruments of freedom and liberty as well as blessings of happiness. A clear conscience gives us peace. We will feel good.

Seeking the Lord's Input in Using Our Agency. We have all been given the light of Christ to help us in the wise use of our agency (see Moroni 7:15–17). And even when the choice seems unclear, we can ask for the Lord's input through sincere prayer. On matters of importance, we can use our own initiative to follow the Lord's counsel: "You must study it out in your mind; then you must ask me if it be right, and if it is right I will cause that your bosom shall burn within you; therefore, you shall feel that it is right. But if it be not right you shall have no such feelings, but you shall have a stupor of thought that shall cause you to forget the thing which is wrong . . ." (D&C 9:8–9).

Prophetic Counsel. Not all decisions will require this kind of spiritual answer-seeking, and so President Gordon B. Hinckley gave us a wonderful formula for making decisions:

> I should like to suggest three standards by which to judge each of the decisions that determine the behavior patterns of your lives. These standards are so simple as to appear elementary, but I believe their faithful observance will provide a set of moral imperatives by which to govern without argument or equivocation each of our actions and which will bring unmatched rewards. They are: 1. Does it enrich the mind? 2. Does it discipline and strengthen the body? 3. Does it nourish the spirit? ("Caesar, Circus, or Christ?" *BYU Speeches of the Year*, Oct. 26, 1965, 4)

Choosing Among Worthwhile Options. Life presents for all of us a series of never-ending choices, some of small scope and some of large but none without consequences. In making the big decisions in our lives, we are not left alone but are entitled to the guidance of the Spirit, for the Lord knows of future events and consequences that we cannot foretell. One man remembers turning to the Lord when faced with a tough choice about how to pursue his career:

> I remember many years ago facing the challenging decision of which graduate school to attend in furthering my professional education. It had been my great fortune and honor to be accepted by several reputable universities, any one of which could have provided a desirable environment for learning. I can recall kneeling in fervent prayer, after much discussion with my wife and following a period of much fasting and

pondering, to ask the Lord's guidance with this important decision concerning our future. The answer was clear and unmistakable. The decision was made. The move was accomplished. A new phase of life began and, as it turned out, there were many unexpected opportunities for service in the Church in the new geographical location, including a calling as a bishop, followed thereafter by a number of stake leadership positions in high councils and stake presidencies. Was this a part of the equation? I believe that it must have been.

Truly the Lord sees the end from the beginning and can lead us to exercise our agency in ways that will bring blessings we could never have foreseen.

Sometimes, when we are faced with more than one good option, the Lord will not influence us toward one or the other because He would be pleased with any decision or because He knows us well enough to know which option we will choose on our own. The Prophet Joseph Smith recorded such a case from the life of Heber C. Kimball: "Brother Heber C. Kimball came to me for counsel, to know whether he should go into the vineyard to proclaim the Gospel, or go to school. I told him he might do either that he should choose, for the Lord would bless him. He chose to go into the vineyard; and immediately went down through the State of New York, into Vermont, his native State. He stopped a short time, and then returned to the city of Ogdensburg, on the St. Lawrence River, where he built up a church of twenty members" (*History of the Church* 2:441). It is instructive that in this case, when a faithful brother was faced with a choice between two worthwhile endeavors, the Prophet acted as would the Lord in respecting the brother's right of moral agency and instructing him to choose either of the available good options. Perhaps, also like the Lord, Joseph was able to discern what Brother Kimball's choice would be from his knowledge of his friend's character. Certainly the twenty converts in Ogdensburg rejoiced at his decision. But if the Lord had wanted Brother Kimball to pursue his education before starting this missionary journey, He would have made that preference clear, rejoicing in Heber's choice to seek heavenly counsel but also respecting his right to ultimately decide for himself.

Of all of our blessings, the freedom to choose and act is most cherished by mankind. Heavenly Father ordained it so because He loves us and seeks our eternal life and happiness. It behooves us to use our agency wisely so that our choices can bring us happiness through the Atonement of the Lord Jesus Christ. We can choose to be firm in the faith and willing to repent. We can choose to keep the commandments, live by the Spirit, and endure to the end. We can choose to be disciples of Jesus Christ, full of hope, full of charity, and with an eye single to the glory of God. We can choose to be patient, generous, kind, virtuous, temperate, humble, diligent, and supportive (rather than envious or given to gossip). We can choose to look for the good, be nurturers, search the scriptures, and be grateful. We can choose to have a positive attitude and live after the manner of happiness. Our choices go on and on. The bottom line is, when we proceed in the framework of eternal principles of truth and happiness, we are choosing to feel good—even when things seem bad.

CHAPTER SIX
THE WISE USE OF TIME

To every thing there is a season, and a time to
every purpose under the heaven: . . . Let us hear the conclusion
of the whole matter: Fear God, and keep his commandments:
for this is the whole duty of man.
—*Ecclesiastes 3:1; 12:13*

Time is a most precious commodity. It can't be stored or saved. It can only be used. The truth is, everyone could use it more wisely. Often we simply let life take us down the river of time. Whatever is going on today we simply partake of. The TV is on, so we watch it. Bargains are at the store, so we go there, whether we need something or not. Yes, we are subject to all things that are going on. However, the pivotal idea about the use of time is that we can choose how to use it—we can plan what we want to have happen and when. There are emergencies from time to time, of course, but we can usually stay in control. If we can control our time, we can control our productivity. Most of all, we'll enjoy life more and feel enhanced self-esteem.

In terms of ultimate goals, the most productive use of time was identified by the Savior: "But seek ye first the kingdom of God, and his righteousness; and all these things shall be added unto you" (Matthew 6:33). If our time is spent fulfilling that commission faithfully and valiantly, then we will have mastered time in the way the Lord has ordained.

Let us make time our ally. We can achieve our goals if we use our time wisely. When we truly gain control of our time, we are in control of our lives, and when our lives are in harmony with our deepest values, we will feel peace. In other words, when we use our time according to our prioritized goals and plans, we'll achieve our objectives and feel successful in our lives. Above all, let us use our time wisely for celestial pursuits, such that we can say, with Paul, on that day of accountability, "I have fought a good fight, I have finished my course, I have kept the faith" (2 Timothy 4:7). We will feel much better about ourselves and be highly productive when we treasure time and use it wisely.

Procrastination. A very special element of time management is overcoming that universal tendency to procrastinate. Procrastination can be generally defined as putting off tasks, duties, or responsibilities of a high priority in favor of other—sometimes easier or more pleasant—activities of a lower priority. We typically use procrastination in the case of less-appealing or more difficult activities. We usually don't "procrastinate" watching our favorite television programs, socializing, or reading a favorite book. Procrastination can have negative effects: stress, loss of a job, bad grades, relationship problems, health difficulties, and many other problems. In spiritual matters, procrastination can be even more problematic. The main cause of procrastination is our own natural self-justifying tendencies: "I'll start that project tomorrow when I have more time—besides, I work better under pressure," or "I'll delay making a will and getting life insurance because there is plenty of time to get that done." Such excuses are obvious rationalizations, but every one of us has used one or more of them from time to time. The more we procrastinate, the harder it seems to be to perform the task or responsibility at hand. One observer made this apt comparison: "Procrastination is likened to the physics concept of inertia—a mass at rest tends to stay at rest." The problem is that our vitality and spiritual well-being depend on action now, lest we find our lamps empty of oil when the hour of judgment comes.

The key to defeating procrastination involves taking control of our own destinies in a prayerful and committed way (see Alma 26:11–12). We can then get organized around realistic goals that can be accomplished in a reasonable time (see D&C 88:119), put together teams of mutually supporting workers that will cooperate in getting things done with focused momentum, and measure progress carefully one milestone after the other. We should also remember to reward ourselves with a little fun for progress made by sending procrastination slinking into the shadows. All these strategies constitute a self-motivating system that takes discipline—but it's worth it, for the rewards are grand.

As you consider how to use your time more effectively, here are a few strategies that might be helpful:

- **Commit time to things that matter most.** Set a few top priority goals for your life, and concentrate on the daily and weekly actions that will bring you closer to the realization of these objectives. Most of the other time-consuming activities can be eliminated or held to a minimum. You can take control of your time if you plan well, remain active and energized with productive tasks, and de-emphasize those things in life that have no lasting value by committing your time to the things that matter most. Remember, as Charles Bixton counseled: "You will never find time for anything. If you want time, you must make it."
- **Use a few wise and proven methods of time management.** Prioritize carefully, and follow through with exactness on what really matters. Delegate wisely by learning the art and science of teamwork and accountability. Those who "do it all" by themselves lose the opportunity to leverage their time and energy and accelerate their success rate through effective teamwork. You can layer your time by deriving multiple benefits from the same activity. An example would be combining business and pleasure on the same trip or using commute time to accomplish important professional tasks. In the "waiting moments" you can have

something to read or write. Sometimes a meditative moment will decrease stress. Moreover, you can make good use of tools such as organizers (print or electronic) and efficient emailing and texting (but not while driving!). Keep meetings to a minimum and make the ones you do have as productive as possible. Above all, you can thwart the enemy—procrastination—by taking charge of your life in a proactive way.

- **Don't forget to have fun.** There is wisdom in staying flexible and resilient and in avoiding becoming enslaved to routine daily tasks. Always, you can make time for your family. Sometimes a little spontaneity can reap a harvest of good memories. At the same time, avoid perfectionism— some things need only to be done adequately, not perfectly. There is an abundance of joy in taking time to relax with a little meditation, exercise, and recreation. That is time used wisely because it will make you more productive in your other pursuits.

- **Remember the Lord's time.** There is wisdom in learning to measure time using a higher clock. We may become so efficient with our mortal time management that we forget to include those things that bring success on a higher plane of existence. Remember to make time for scripture study, family activities, personal time, expressions of love, and service. These are most valuable uses of time. Take time to pray—expressing gratitude, asking for guidance, and seeking wisdom in the use of time. The Lord will bless you richly.

Perhaps the best one-line summary of managing your time, especially when it comes to matters of spiritual progress and development, is the following statement from King Benjamin: "And now, if you believe all these things see that ye do them" (Mosiah 4:10). We never know how long our probationary span of mortality will last. Let us not procrastinate but prepare ourselves each day as if it were our last. Our happiness and joy—and that of our families—altogether depend upon it.

CHAPTER SEVEN
IF WE ARE PREPARED, WE WILL PROSPER

Yea, a voice crying—Prepare ye the way of the Lord, prepare ye the supper of the Lamb, make ready for the Bridegroom.
—*D&C 65:3*

The precursor to success in human endeavor can usually be found in preparation. There are many factors that determine success: vision, desire, commitment, and a host of others. When the vision and desire are in place, preparation becomes the master. Preparation precedes power. Confucius wisely said, "A man who does not think and plan long ahead will find trouble right at his door." But if you are prepared, you will not suffer from anxiety—or as the Lord expressed it, "If ye are prepared ye shall not fear" (D&C 38:30).

Preparation has a price. It takes time, effort, dedication, and often sacrifice in order to prepare well. Many want to be the best, become the champion, and win the prize—and a litany of other reasons to achieve could be listed. The question is, how many want to prepare to be the best and, thus, become the champion and win the prize? Preparation becomes the key to success along with the perseverance and dedication to see it through. Such is the case in dealing with trials and frustrations—we must prepare well, and then we will be better able to handle our problems. Let us consider the following as we prepare every needful thing:

- **Preparation Begins in the Mind and Heart.** Like an eagle spreading its wings, you can open up your capacity.

You can make yourself internally capable of doing all that is required. Louis Pasteur's famous dictum comes to mind: "Chance favors only those minds which are prepared." When surprises occur, you will feel secure because of your preparation. Furthermore, you can prepare an internal vision—an uncompromising vision of being successful at the objectives you have committed yourself to achieve, especially the objective to prepare to meet God. To engage in that process, you can commit to correct principles of honesty, integrity, sacrifice, and service. Prepare your attitudes ahead of time, deciding to be positive, flexible, resilient, resourceful in dealing with obstacles along the way, and relentless in affirming your ability to succeed.

• **Preparation Includes Certain Key Actions That Are Indispensable.** Then you must design and lay out a detailed plan for achieving what you desire. What are the target goals, objectives, deadlines, and milestones? In defining these, you must be incorrigibly realistic, never committing to expectations that are beyond the attainable, lest quality and productivity be sacrificed on the altar of dreamland fantasies. You can select target dates along the way to be sure your preparation is on schedule. You will feel joy when you surpass your own expectations. Like an experienced pilot, follow a detailed checklist of things you need to do in your preparation. Some items on your list might be scripture study, meaningful prayer, magnifying your calling and eternal roles, and caring for loved ones. Nothing feels so good as when you check off the things you need to do. Of course, you must also prepare for contingencies and unexpected surprises. Playing a shrewd game of "what if" will help you keep unanticipated road bumps to a minimum, especially if you organize all needful resources, build a motivated and effective team equal to the task, and put in place the means to evaluate and track your progress along the way. By measuring and evaluating as you go, the milestones—one after the other—can be identified and midcourse corrections completed as needed.

- **Preparation Is an Ongoing Process.** One you have designed and initiated a plan for success, the preparation is not over. After each triumph, you must stand ready to do it all over again. Preparation is not a one-time thing. It continues unabated as you meet unexpected detours, add new players to the team, upgrade and expand your objectives, and raise the bar of excellence along the way. Ralph Waldo Emerson observed, "The future belongs to those who prepare for it—and who work for it and live for it." Make a covenant with yourself to engage your highest capacities, muster your full measure of strength, and rise to your greatest potential. Rehearse as you go, practicing dry runs in advance, simulating the campaign ahead of the deployment. The key is to cultivate expectations continually. In this way you can prepare to reach the summit of your expectations, neutralizing any fear of success, eliminating any doubts about your potential and ability, and galvanizing your power to succeed—intellectually, emotionally, and spiritually.

Prophetic Counsel. In a talk entitled, "If Ye Are Prepared Ye Shall Not Fear," President Gordon B. Hinckley stated:

> The Lord has said, "If ye are prepared ye shall not fear" (D&C 38:30).
>
> The primary preparation is also set forth in the Doctrine and Covenants, wherein it says, "Wherefore, stand ye in holy places, and be not moved, until the day of the Lord come" (D&C 87:8). . . .
>
> We can so live that we can call upon the Lord for His protection and guidance. This is a first priority. We cannot expect His help if we are unwilling to keep His commandments. . . .
>
> We can heed warnings. . . . I have faith . . . that the Lord will bless us, and watch over us, and

assist us if we walk in obedience to His light, His gospel, and His commandments. (*Ensign,* Nov. 2005, 60)

Our most important preparation in this life is preparing to meet our God (see Alma 34:32). A plan for our spiritual survival is therefore more vital to the well-being of our souls than any temporal preparedness plan. But indeed the same guidelines we've been given for temporal preparation can be applied to spiritual preparation because the Lord has said, "All things unto me are spiritual, and not at any time have I given unto you a law which was temporal" (D&C 29:34). The temporal and the spiritual are connected. When our Church leaders encourage us to prepare for emergencies by having food and other supplies on hand, they are not just asking us to follow a temporal law; they are asking us to follow the Spirit. So how can we use temporal preparation guidelines to become spiritually prepared?

The Eternal 72-Hour Kit. Many of us are working on our physical 72-hour kits in order to be prepared for emergencies. But we also need an eternal 72-hour kit in order to be spiritually prepared. What do we put in this kit? Let's look at some symbolic possibilities:

• **Food and Water**. We are counseled to have food and water in our temporal 72-hour kit. Our corresponding spiritual 72-hour kit should contain nourishment of a different kind. The Lord said, "I am the bread of life: he that cometh to me shall never hunger; and he that believeth on me shall never thirst" (John 6:35). Every week we partake of the bread of life and the living water of the gospel through the ordinance of the sacrament. We prepare ourselves spiritually every time we partake of the sacrament and renew our covenants with the Lord.
• **Shelter**. We are counseled to have adequate shelter in times of emergency. Our temporal kit may contain tents

and coverings for our family. Our eternal 72-hour kit might include the shelter of our righteous homes, our ward or stake, and even the temple. We have been counseled to "gather together, and stand in holy places" (D&C 101:22; see also D&C 45:32; 87:8)—meaning the stakes, temples, and homes of Zion. If we are spiritually prepared, then we will have a spiritual shelter at all times under the protecting influence of the Lord.

• **Clothing**. We are counseled to have adequate clothing in times of emergency. What kind of clothing do we have in our eternal 72-hour kit? We are admonished to "put on the whole armour of God" (Ephesians 6:11; see also D&C 27:15)—"Above all, taking the shield of faith" (Ephesians 6:16; see also D&C 27:17). When we don the armor of God and exercise our faith, we will then be better prepared spiritually to withstand the tribulations that are upon us and that will surely be increased in the future. Another type of clothing for our spiritual survival kit might be the temple garment, symbolizing the sacred covenants entered into in the Lord's holy house. As we faithfully remain true to our temple covenants, we will be prepared for and protected against the trials and temptations that will come.

• **Communication System**. We are counseled to have an efficient communication system on hand in times of emergency—radios and the like. What do we have in our eternal 72-hour kit that corresponds to that? Could it be prayer? That is the Lord's communication system—in times of ease as well as in times of emergency. As we learn from the Bible Dictionary, "Prayer is the act by which the will of the Father and the will of the child are brought into correspondence [or communication] with each other" ("Prayer," Bible Dictionary).

• **Compass**. We are counseled to have a compass in our physical 72-hour kit. What would correspond to that in our spiritual kit? It would be the scriptures—the word of God. If we follow the iron rod we will never be off course. Indeed, "whosoever will may lay hold upon the word of God, which is quick and powerful, which shall . . . lead the man of Christ in a strait and narrow course across that everlasting gulf of misery which is prepared to engulf the wicked—And land their souls, yea, their immortal souls, at the right hand of God in the kingdom of heaven" (Helaman 3:29–30). In the words of Nephi, "The words of Christ will tell you all things what ye should do" (2 Nephi 32:3).

• **Flashlight.** We are counseled to have a flashlight in our physical 72-hour kit. In our spiritual 72-hour kit we can light our path with the words of the living prophets of God—as conveyed through general conference and the *Ensign* and *Liahona* magazines. If we will listen to and follow these illuminating teachings, then we will be spiritually prepared from hour to hour. Said the Lord: "What I the Lord have spoken, I have spoken, and I excuse not myself; and though the heavens and the earth pass away, my word shall not pass away, but shall all be fulfilled, whether by mine own voice or by the voice of my servants, it is the same" (D&C 1:38). In this context, we can also remember the words of the Psalmist: "Thy word is a lamp unto my feet, and a light unto my path" (Psalm 119:105).

• **Fuel.** We are counseled to store fuel for heating and cooking in an emergency. What do we have of this kind in our spiritual 72-hour kit? Is it not the warmth of close relationships? Families are to stand together in unity and love, and strong friendships provide additional support. We are to enjoy the warmth and love of close relationships at all times—especially in times of urgency or disaster. The Lord reminded Joseph Smith in times of tribulation: "Thy friends do stand by thee, and they shall hail thee again with warm hearts and friendly hands" (D&C 121:9; see also D&C 38:27). The same promise holds for us all.

• **First-Aid Supplies.** We are counseled to include a first-aid kit in our emergency supplies—medicines and materials to be used in healing wounds, relieving pain, and curing ailments.

In our spiritual 72-hour kit, we should include the "balm of Gilead" (see Jeremiah 8:22), or the healing power of the Atonement. Our spiritual preparation includes accepting the healing process of the Atonement of Jesus Christ into our lives. When we do this, there is no emergency that can move us from our moorings in the gospel.

We are counseled to be upbeat and positive in times of emergency—to foster an attitude of hope. That is the key to following through successfully with our preparations. The Lord tells us many times in the scriptures to "be of good cheer." The gospel provides the key of good cheer. It is the key to the eternal mansions available through obedience to gospel principles. The Lord said, "In the world ye shall have tribulation: but be of good cheer; I have overcome the world" (John 16:33). And furthermore: "Be not troubled . . . the promises which have been made unto you shall be fulfilled" (D&C 45:35). The signs of the times may be troubling, but let us prepare instead of being troubled, for these signs mean that the promises of the Lord will be fulfilled for each of us and our families.

President Thomas S. Monson counseled: "One day, each of us will run out of tomorrows. Let us not put off what is most important. . . . Preparation is hard work but absolutely essential for our progress" ("In Search of Treasure," *Liahona,* May 2003, 19–22). Faith is the essence of preparation and the power of action. Again, the words of the Lord: "If ye are prepared ye shall not fear" (D&C 38:30).

Preparation is more important than we sometimes realize. It is paramount that we make preparation in all things a permanent part of our lives. Preparation takes consummate organization so that there is adequate time available to achieve our goals. With an attitude of masterful preparation, we will feel more in control and can expect greater success. It is better to look ahead and prepare than to look back and regret. Therefore, let us all make it a goal to prepare well and enjoy the blessings of joy and success in life, now and in the hereafter.

CHAPTER EIGHT
HOPE: OPTIMISM TOWARD THE FUTURE

Let thy mercy, O LORD, be upon us,
according as we hope in thee.
—*Psalm 33:22*

Our anticipation and expectation for things to be good or better in our lives is called hope. Our hope is based upon the Lord Jesus Christ and upon the plan of happiness and eternal life, which God promised to the faithful before the world began (see Titus 1:2). Hope provides us with a sense of confidence in looking forward to a realization of our most worthy aspirations in life. When we lose hope, life becomes difficult in every sense. A life without hope is empty; but a life filled with hope is a life filled with light and meaning. We can start with faith in Jesus Christ and confidence in the gospel plan of redemption. Cultivate an attitude of being optimistic, appreciative, and grateful—while at the same time using practical wisdom in developing a lifestyle based on positive and uplifting hope. We choose. If we live hopefully and then cheerfully do all we can to rise to our potential, the arm of the Lord will be extended to us (see D&C 123:17).

Prophetic Counsel. Hope is based on gospel truths and not on the things of the world. As Elder Russell M. Nelson has said, "The gospel of Jesus Christ provides hope for all in this wailing world. 'Now, what do we hear in the gospel which we have received? A voice of gladness! A voice of mercy from heaven; and a voice of truth out of the earth; glad tidings for the dead;

a voice of gladness for the living and the dead; glad tidings of great joy' (D&C 128:19)" (*The Gateway We Call Death* [Salt Lake City: Deseret Book, 1995], 108–9).

Many people in this world appear to be dejected, depressed, and in a state of hopelessness. Where there is no hope there is no happiness or joy. The causes for hopelessness vary, but the solution is always possible in and through our Savior Jesus Christ. If we build upon His rock, we can stand tall and be lifted by hope. Things get better sooner or later. We should always take a step away from the situation and look at it objectively (emotional feelings often make one unable to assess situations properly). People in the darkest chasms of despair can become full of hope as they apply the principles and teachings of the gospel consistently and with devotion. Remember, "with God all things are possible" (Matthew 19:26).

Hope has power to enrich our lives with joy and happiness. Mormon taught us about the blessings of hope and love, together with their associated virtues: "And the remission of sins bringeth meekness, and lowliness of heart; and because of meekness and lowliness of heart cometh the visitation of the Holy Ghost, which Comforter filleth with hope and perfect love, which love endureth by diligence unto prayer, until the end shall come, when all the saints shall dwell with God" (Moroni 8:26). When we depend upon God and have an attitude of hope (enjoying an optimistic attitude towards the future due to our knowledge of God's plan), we will feel the Spirit and have joy. It is impossible to "feel good" without the Spirit. But with the Spirit, we are lifted up in joy and confidence: "But they that wait upon the Lord shall renew their strength; they shall mount up with wings as eagles; they shall run, and not be weary; and they shall walk, and not faint" (Isaiah 40:31). With hope we are ready. We can be better. We can have a better day.

Happiness and joy can begin with a good attitude full of optimism and hope. A hopeful attitude attracts us to the conditions and possibilities of joy and happiness. It is the way we choose to live (see 2 Nephi 2:27; 5:27). As long as our values are rooted in truth and correct principles, our attitudes will affect our level of happiness almost more than anything else— because as we think, so are we. "Most people are about as happy as they make up their minds to be," said Abraham Lincoln. And the wise man of the scriptures stated: "For as he thinketh in his heart, so is he" (Proverbs 23:7).

Look Ahead to Joy. One couple shared the following strategy of hope and positive thinking:

> My wife and I have devised a saying that we rehearse together rather frequently. It simply says, "Don't look back on sorrow—look ahead to joy." When circumstances begin to cast a shadow over the pathway of life and we begin to give voice to discouragement, then one or the other of us retrieves that little saying and, with a smile, recites it. Then we both nod with understanding and say it together, or sing it to a little tune we have developed: "Don't look back on sorrow—look ahead to joy." There is really no other choice in life. Through the hope of the gospel we can indeed look forward to joy. Thank heaven for loved ones who can serve together and make the pathway of life bearable. Over the years my wife and I have added another sentence to our saying: "Don't look back on sorrow—look ahead to joy. Hand in hand we'll go, finding our tomorrow, for we know we'll always go in love."

The burdens of life can serve a constructive purpose: "All these things shall give thee experience, and shall be for thy good," the Lord said to the Prophet Joseph (D&C 122:7). At times our spirit of courage can wane and our hope can slacken—almost as if we were without life. Those are the times when the Comforter can breathe new hope into us. Truly the Lord can revive us on a daily basis—if we will allow Him to do so. "O the hope of Israel, the saviour thereof in time of trouble" (Jeremiah 14:8) is how Jeremiah expressed the healing mission of the Redeemer, whose will it is to teach us the principles of righteousness and joy.

Hope in Christ gives us power to deal with life. Through hope we increase our faith in a positive and joyful way, for the "hope of the righteous shall be gladness . . ." (Proverbs 10:28). We *know* that sooner or later things will be better. In our desires, thoughts, and deeds we act on trust and hope: "Blessed is the man that trusteth in the LORD, and whose hope the LORD is" (Jeremiah 17:7). In all things we cherish the counsel of Nephi and strive to follow it with devotion: "Wherefore, ye must press forward with a steadfastness in Christ, having a perfect brightness of hope, and a love of God and of all men. Wherefore, if ye shall press forward, feasting upon the word of Christ, and endure to the end, behold, thus saith the Father: Ye shall have eternal life" (2 Nephi 31:20).

We see that hope is an active quality, resulting in a condition of "pressing forward." We see that hope is consistent and unwavering—"steadfast." We see that hope fills us with light and love. Above all, we see that our enduring hope, anchored in the word of Christ, leads to the magnificent blessing of eternal life. Our mortal journey is brief in the eternal expanse of existence. Though things at times seem challenging and sometimes sad, we can take comfort in knowing that "a more excellent hope" (Ether 12:32) lifts our vision to the bright side of our purpose and destiny. The fabric of a saintly life is woven out of the threads of hope—mingled with those of faith, meekness, and charity (see D&C 12:8). With hope and its attendant qualities, we can strengthen the foundation upon which we build a lifetime of valor and obedience—and look forward to a future of eternal life and everlasting joy.

CHAPTER NINE
GRATITUDE

And he who receiveth all things with thankfulness
shall be made glorious; and the things of this earth shall be
added unto him, even an hundred fold, yea, more.
—D&C 78:19

What is the key for looking on the bright side of life? It is cultivating an attitude of gratitude. Gratitude is a cardinal virtue and a catalyst for change. Gratitude is usually felt when you understand and appreciate someone or something. There is nothing quite so beautiful and wholesome as the experience of gratitude. It blesses both the giver and the receiver. An attitude of gratitude enhances our lives, for it enables us to begin to see the things that matter most. Gratitude changes our attitude and behavior. We seek to bless and serve, and we have greater hope—even in times of adversity and challenge.

When we live in thanksgiving daily, our minds are filled with thoughts of gratitude for all things. Every part of our lives is a blessing from God—to see, to hear, to smell, to touch, to taste, to breathe, to swallow, to walk—everything. The earth in all its beauty pleases the eye and gladdens the soul: the mountains, the rivers, the lakes, the magnificent formations, the flowers, the trees, and everything that dwells here on earth, including the animals in all their beauty and splendor. We can be grateful if we have eyes that see and hearts that feel.

We should all live in thanksgiving and gratitude at all times. When that happens, we become selfless rather than selfish, meaning we are always looking out to bless others rather than simply to satisfy our own wants and desires. We feel better about ourselves and feel better about each and every day. We begin to taste the fruits of our labors and enjoy the spirit of joy and happiness.

For many, happiness in mortality turns out to be fleeting because the perceived source of happiness is rooted in a worldly value system. We can never find happiness in mortality without the eternal perspective of the plan of happiness. The eternal perspective gives credence to mortality as part of an eternal landscape. Life can be wonderful as we seek eternal truths and then choose to keep the Lord's commandments. To be humble and devout players on this grand stage of life makes of us seekers of happiness rather than simply participants in the mortal experience. "Men are, that they might have joy," stated the Prophet Lehi (see 2 Nephi 2:25). And that joy and happiness flows from seeking the will of the Father and following in the footsteps of the Son. You can feel better and look on the bright side—even when things seem bad. A life anchored in hope and gratitude is destined to yield a harvest of joy and happiness.

Prophetic Counsel. The Apostle Paul counseled us to give "thanks always for all things unto God and the Father in the name of our Lord Jesus Christ" (Ephesians 5:20). King Benjamin taught that the blessings of God are so magnificent and all-encompassing that you would still be indebted to Him, even if you should "render all the thanks and praise which your whole soul has power to possess, to that God who has created you, and has kept and preserved you, and has caused that ye should rejoice, and has granted that ye should live in peace one with another" (Mosiah 2:20). The Lord blesses us far beyond the measure of our performance and expressed gratitude because He loves us. President Joseph F. Smith stated: "The grateful man sees so much in the world to be thankful for, and with him the good outweighs the evil. Love overpowers jealousy, and light drives darkness out of his life. Pride destroys our gratitude and sets up selfishness in its place. How much happier we are in the presence of a grateful and loving soul, and how careful we should be to cultivate, through the medium of a prayerful life, a thankful attitude toward God and man!" (*Gospel Doctrine: Selections from the Sermons and Writings of Joseph F. Smith*, comp. John A. Widtsoe [Salt Lake City: Deseret Book, 1919], 263).

How can we remember to be more grateful? Here are four simple but effective strategies:

- **Remember That Gratitude Spreads Under Its Own Power**. By showing gratitude to others, we touch their hearts and inspire in them a desire to be grateful. Gratitude sows joy in the receiver and the giver. When you help others see their blessings, they will have a greater desire to do good.
- **Remember That Gratitude Brings Its Own Rewards**. These rewards include feelings of confidence and self-worth, unity and togetherness in families and groups, a greater capacity to appreciate the good, and enhanced stature as a leader. Gratitude is an element of leadership that attracts others to follow your example.
- **Remember That Gratitude Starts with the Little Things**.
  - **Look around**—Open your vision to the good and look for the best in others. Often by looking for things to be grateful for, you will find that you have blessings in abundance. And you will discover at the same time that there are always people who have more trials and problems than you do. *Count your many blessings.*
  - **Catch others doing good**—By catching others doing good and expressing gratitude to them for it, you open the way for greater happiness and joy in life.
  - **Say it**—Express gratitude on a regular basis to your family, friends, and coworkers. Write a "thank you" note every month (or more frequently if you can) to someone who has blessed your life.
  - **Ask for it**—Desire a grateful heart as a blessing from the Lord.

• **Remember that Being Grateful to the Lord Brings Him Joy.** The Lord expects us to feel and express thanksgiving and gratitude. When we fail to acknowledge God in all things, we offend Him (see D&C 59:21; Mosiah 26:39). As we express gratitude, we can experience blessings of the Spirit (see D&C 11:12–13; Galatians 5:22–23).

The grateful person has a refreshing way of looking at the world. The principle is clear: when you feel grateful, you will often show it through service. And you will be amazed how others will follow your example. That is the miracle of gratitude. Certainly one of the hallmarks of a disciple of the Savior is a lifestyle that reflects gratitude and thanksgiving. Gratitude lets you look on the bright side—which is truly the authentic side of life—because life was meant to be filled with joy, now and forever.

CHAPTER TEN
CHOOSE JOY TODAY

Adam fell that men might be; and men are,
that they might have joy.
—2 Nephi 2:25

Life can be difficult. Life is full of adversity. But the purpose of this life is that we might have joy (see 2 Nephi 2:25)— and not just in the eternities but also in the here and now. Life can and should be an enjoyable experience, even fun. To make life beautiful, enjoyable, and fulfilling, we must build our value system around the gospel of Jesus Christ. As we keep the commandments, we will find happiness as the reward for our righteousness. This is what we should seek in life.

Even though we have lasting joy as our goal, sometimes when we receive blessings and things are going well, we forget the Lord due to the easiness of the way (see 2 Nephi 28:24; Helaman 12:2). We often take our gifts and blessings for granted until we lose them. This is why the Lord has to remind us continually through chastening. Knowing that we tend to be mercurial in nature will help us understand the problems we face. We can make adjustments so that our coping skills will improve and our emotions can be kept in check. We can view our challenges from an eternal perspective and look on the bright side as we endure faithfully to the end.

Prophetic Counsel. Elder Marvin J. Ashton put it this way: "In whatever circumstance we may find ourselves, whether in the midst of tragedy, the pain of misconduct, or merely the daily struggle to live the life of a faithful Latter-day Saint, we must remember 'the race is not to the swift, nor the battle to the strong, but he that endureth to the end shall be saved'" (*Be of Good Cheer* [Salt Lake City: Deseret Book, 1987], 21). Elder Neal A. Maxwell had the following to say concerning meekness and thanksgiving during times of adversity: "Determining whether we will live myopically and selfishly or live now for eternity is a fundamental decision that colors every day of daily life. To live a life of 'thanksgiving daily' (Alma 34:38) while in the midst of adversity and its tutorials is impossible without a degree of meekness" (*Meek and Lowly* [Salt Lake City: Deseret Book, 1987], 4).

Feeling good, even when things seem bad, is a function of how we look at life and apply the principles of eternity day by day. Here are a few things to remember as you seek to generate more joy in your life:

- **Life Is What You Choose to Make It.** Remember that you can choose your responses to life, including all your governing attitudes. Thus you can have an attitude of hope, with the conviction that sooner or later things can and will be better (see Ether 12:4). With that kind of attitude, you can be positive and triumphantly defeat any self-fulfilling negative outlook. At the same time, you can choose to uphold your standards, values, and principles in exemplary ways and cultivate a long-term vision of life. Seek lasting joy rather than short-term pleasures, and you will find the abundance of spiritual wealth rather than the emptiness of shallow dreams.
- **Life Is This Very Moment.** An important truth to remember in your quest for joy is that you needn't wait to enjoy life. You can enjoy the journey today. Life is now—not "out there" but "in here." Life is made up of all the moment-by-moment feelings, happenings, and opportunities that occur in your world. You can think of each moment as a special act of living, or you can think

of it as a burden. It's all in how you respond. Life is a miracle, a state of vitality, a feeling of "aliveness" that has its own wondrous, self-sustaining energy of well-being. Even at times of illness and depression, you can hold onto each moment of living as one more opportunity to enjoy the sunrise, to watch the sunset, to marvel at nature's handiwork, to hold the hand of a loved one, or to kindle a soul-deep hope for better times to come. In all of this, you can still keep life simple, avoiding the shackles of overprogramming or overcommitting yourself. Too many "things" make life hectic and sometimes unbearable. Keep each moment pure and simple. "And see that all these things are done in wisdom and order; for it is not requisite that a man should run faster than he has strength" (Mosiah 4:27). Above all, stay healthy—eating well, getting adequate rest, and exercising regularly. It's your choice, and the blessings are myriad for complying.

• **Life Is Enriched through Service to Others.** Life is togetherness. Everyone can have togetherness, even a person who has no immediate family or relatives. How? That person can still help and serve others out of a deep commitment to humanity, out of a deep sense of obligation to make this a better world. Similarly, you can enrich your life by looking beyond yourself to the opportunities for serving others. You can seek to build up the kingdom of God, finding joy and glory in being an instrument in the hand of the Lord to help people come unto Christ (see Joseph Smith Translation Matthew 6:38; Alma 29:9–10). The joy of service is exquisite (see Alma 36:24).

• **Life Is an Exhilarating Climb Upward, One Step at a Time.** What does it take to rise to our potential? To begin with, we can come to understand that life is an affirmation of our highest prospects and possibilities. Life is nothing if not an opportunity to rise on the wings of self-transcendence and self-mastery to the highest level of which we are capable. Seen in this context, life is always a blessing and a positive challenge. With that knowledge in mind, prepare well and organize yourself for life's journey (see D&C 88:119). Part of the joy in life is getting ready to climb higher. You can communicate with care and be true to your promises, knowing that joy will come as you follow through with your commitments. Above all, you can "do it now." Procrastination ends up causing us to waste more energy being frustrated than we would spend just getting the job done in the first place. There is joy in savoring the good consequences. There are grand rewards that come when things are done well and goals are achieved. Finally, you can make life a spiritual experience. Life on earth is a training ground for a better life to come in the hereafter. Nothing acts with more persuasion to quell the narrow appetites of a mortal nature than the desire, hope, and faith to qualify for an eternal life in which the cares of this world are replaced with the glories of eternal lives in the celestial kingdom (see 2 Nephi 9:39).

Finding Joy Today. The following excerpt is a list of ideas for finding joy today, in spite of whatever happened yesterday and whatever may happen tomorrow.

"Just for Today"

1. Just for today, I will try to live through this day only and not set far-reaching goals in an effort to overcome all my problems at once. I know I can do something for twelve hours that would appall me if I had to keep it up for a lifetime.

2. Just for today, I will try to be happy. Abraham Lincoln said, "Most folks are about as happy as they make up their minds to be." He was right. I will not dwell on thoughts that depress me. I will chase them from my mind and replace them with happy thoughts.

3. Just for today, I will adjust myself to what is. I will face reality. I will try to change those things I can and accept those things I cannot change.

4. Just for today, I will try to improve my mind. I will not be a mental loafer. I will force myself to read something that requires effort, thought, and concentration.

5. Just for today, I will exercise my soul in three ways. I will do a good deed for somebody without letting them know it. (If they find out I did it, it won't count.) I will do at least two things that I know I should do but have been putting off. I will not show anyone that my feelings are hurt; they may be hurt, but today I will not show it.

6. Just for today, I will be agreeable. I will look as good as I can, dress becomingly, talk softly, act courteously, and speak ill of no one. Just for today, I'll not try to improve anybody except myself.

7. Just for today, I will have a program. I may not follow it exactly, but I will have it, thereby saving myself from two pests—hurry and indecision.

8. Just for today, I will have a quiet half hour to relax alone. During this time, I will reflect on my behavior to try to get better perspective on my life.

9. Just for today, I will be unafraid. I will gather the courage to do what is right and will take the responsibility for my own actions. I will expect nothing from the world, but I will realize that as I give to the world, the world will give to me. (Author Unknown; in *Especially for Mormons,* vol. 5, comp. Stan & Sharon Miller and Sherm & Peg Fugal [Provo, Utah: Kellirae Arts year], 168–9.)

You can choose to have a great day and a great life. Life is a gift from God, and its purpose is that we might have joy. All of us can welcome the following advice: "You choose. You choose to make life beautiful and joyful. You are in charge. You can choose to be understanding and kind, to treat people with consideration. You can pass good deeds along. You can help every person you meet have a better day. You can make a difference in their lives as well as yours."

If you decide to choose joy today and every day, you will

feel fulfilled. Life will be sweet. Make a commitment today to live life to the fullest and enjoy your time on earth. Then you can feel good, even when things seem bad.

PART TWO:
SAFE PASSAGE OVER
STORMY SEAS

In the strength of the Lord thou canst do all things.
—Alma 20:4

The challenges and difficulties of this life are not easy. We should not expect smooth sailing every day of our lives. Like Nephi, Alma, and all the great examples in the scriptures, we will trust in the Lord, knowing that He will guide us safely over the stormy seas of life and provide a way for us to accomplish our tasks here upon the earth.

Elder Jeffrey R. Holland taught,

> Note the kinds of problems Alma said the Atonement would remedy—pain, affliction, sickness, sorrow, temptation, and infirmities of every kind, as well as spiritual sin and physical death. This doctrine is central to the full meaning of the mission and ministry of the Lord Jesus Christ. Most Christians believe that, based upon repentance, the Atonement of Christ will redeem humankind from the final consequences of sin and death. But only those who receive the restored gospel, including the Book of Mormon, know how thoroughly the Atonement heals and helps with so many more categories of disappointment and heartache here and now, in time as well as in eternity. In this life as well as the next, Christ "restoreth my

soul" and administers "goodness and mercy . . .
all the days of my life" (Psalm 23:3, 6). (*Christ
and the New Covenant: The Messianic Message
of the Book of Mormon* [Salt Lake City: Deseret
Book, 1997], 113)

The difficulties we face in this life can cause frustration,
heartache, and heartbreak. We must remember that these
challenges constitute one of the reasons why we came to
earth—we came to be tested. But we should also remember that
the purpose of our existence is that we might have joy (see 2
Nephi 2:25). We can find happiness and feel good, even when
things seem unbearable.

Part two is arranged in three sections: Overcoming, Coping,
and Focusing.

CHAPTER ELEVEN
OVERCOMING SELFISHNESS

And now abideth faith, hope, charity, these three;
but the greatest of these is charity.
—1 Corinthians 13:13

Of all the destructive forces in a person's character, nothing is quite so devastating as selfishness. It cankers the soul and destroys other people. Selfishness raises havoc in marriage and makes communication almost nonexistent. It is also the cause of other grievous problems, such as lust, greed, and unrighteous dominion. Of all the negative traits of society and individuals, selfishness is the one we must all work on to overcome. The antidote to this terrible plague is charity—which can never fail. The two are diametrically opposed. In the presence of charity, selfishness vanishes. The Apostle Paul put it most eloquently: "Charity suffereth long, and is kind; charity envieth not; charity vaunteth not itself, is not puffed up" (1 Corinthians 13:4). We can all strive with enduring devotion to purge every ounce of selfishness from our lives so that charity may take its rightful place and provide the foundation for our spiritual salvation. And of course, in cultivating charity in our lives, we will automatically feel good. And thus we see that this business of "feeling good" is tied and bound completely to living the gospel of Jesus Christ. There is no other way.

Understanding Selfishness. Whenever we focus our hearts on ourselves rather than on the well-being of others—whether it be to acquire fame or station or possessions—we suffer from selfishness. Selfishness destroys lives. It destroys souls, and we should avoid selfishness as if it were a plague (see D&C 121:35–36) because it is an aspect of the grievous sin of pride. Pride is and has ever been the downfall of all the unrighteous. Satan uses prideful ambition to snare us and lead us away captive. Only by thinking of others and their welfare first can we ever root out our selfish tendencies (see 3 Nephi 6:15–16).

Prophetic Counsel. President Hinckley defined liberation from the effects of selfishness: "The antidote for selfishness is service, a reaching out to those about us—those in the home and those beyond the walls of the home. A child who grows in a home where there is a selfish, grasping father is likely to develop those tendencies in his own life. On the other hand, a child who sees his father and mother forgo comforts for themselves as they reach out to those in distress, will likely follow the same pattern when he or she grows to maturity" (*Teachings of Gordon B. Hinckley* [Salt Lake City: Deseret Book, 1997], 583).

Selfishness breeds alienation, rancor, greed, envy, and anger. Why would anyone, therefore, commit to a life of selfishness, unless he or she is blind to the inevitable outcomes? Clear vision dismisses selfishness. Consider the following suggestions for clearing your vision and replacing selfishness with charity:

- **Understand that you don't have to put others down in order to be good or successful yourself.** In this world of competition on every corner and venue of life, it seems as though people feel they must put others down to exonerate themselves—and this is surely the influence of the devil and our carnal desires showing through. Looking for the good in others will make you a happier person by giving you a more positive outlook on life. Everyone has some good. You can praise them for it. You can seek to lift others and set aside any tendency for self-aggrandizement.

• **Be content with the success and achievements of others**. Having more than others or being better than others does not ensure happiness. You don't need to be in competition for all things. You can find joy in helping others succeed. Alma, for example, was overjoyed with the success of the sons of Mosiah. He records, "But I do not joy in my own success alone, but my joy is more full because of the success of my brethren, who have been up to the land of Nephi. Behold, they have labored exceedingly, and have brought forth much fruit; and how great shall be their reward! Now, when I think of the success of these my brethren my soul is carried away, even to the separation of it from the body, as it were, so great is my joy" (Alma 29:14–16). With such an attitude of love for your fellowmen, you, too, can find joy in the success of others. It is so refreshing and joyful to praise others. Try it—you will love it.

• **Try to think of others' needs and desires instead of our own**. Be concerned with others and their happiness. Such concern will turn your thoughts away from self and bring greater joy into your life. One person recalled this principle in action in his life: "I remember the day when things all seemed to fall apart. I was miserable. Those thoughts of 'Why me?' 'What have I done to deserve this?' and 'This isn't fair!' echoed in my mind and heart as I cried and prayed. Needless to say, I was feeling horrible. While praying, I received the prompting: 'Forget yourself and go bless someone.' I immediately went and visited my aging mother, and the Spirit brought joy and happiness to my soul. It made all the difference, and I felt terrific." Seeking to help others and bless their lives will root selfishness out of your heart and replace it with genuine love for others.

Building Airplanes. One father remembers a life-changing event that occurred when he realized he was putting his own desires before those of his young son:

Everyone at one time or another displays selfishness. I am guilty. It truly is one thing we all have to work on. I remember the day I decided to quit thinking of myself so much and start thinking of others. I had come home a few minutes early from work because it had been a hard day and I was tired. I needed a little time for myself before dinner. I was sitting in my big easy chair at my desk reading that part of the newspaper that matters most—the sports section. Just as I was relaxing, my cute, red-headed, four-year-old son came up and said, "Daddy, let's build some airplanes." I replied, "Oh son, Daddy is tired. We'll do it later." As only a four-year-old can be, he was relentless. He begged and pleaded. I was selfish. I needed rest. I . . . I . . . I . . . Finally I said in exasperation, "We'll do it when I'm good and ready. Now, leave Daddy alone for a minute."

As he left, I saw a little tear slide down his cheek. I felt horrible. I was a lousy, selfish father. I ran after him and said, "We'll build them right now. We'll build them right now." He smiled, and we built paper airplanes and flew them off our deck. We had a great time together. I made a commitment that day. When I walked into our home, I was King Daddy—like King Benjamin, servant of all—and would always think of the family first, never myself.

As we learn to overcome our selfish tendencies, we will truly find ourselves. We will learn that putting others and their well-being first will drown out selfishness and lead to true charity and happiness. This does not mean we ignore things that need to be changed, tolerate improper behavior, or become permissive, relinquishing values or standards. It means we seek the well-being of all, including ourselves. In doing so, we learn to see things from a different and more pleasing perspective, as the following story illustrates. One man remembers an event in the Caribbean that will not soon be forgotten:

> It was a beautiful spring day in a resort location where several colleagues and I were participating in a business retreat. Two of us were walking along the streets of the city to rejoin our wives and other family members when, all at once, we came upon a teenage boy who seemed to be disoriented and in distress. As we passed by, he looked at us with a glance that suggested a combination of fear and longing. His arms reached out in a beckoning way to the pedestrians around him. He seemed to be challenged in multiple ways. Without stopping, we instinctively circumvented the spot where he was standing and silently continued on our way. Then our pace slackened. Suddenly, my friend stopped and turned around. He walked the few steps back toward the young man and spoke to him. "What can we do to help?" was the question. The young man seemed to be somewhat relieved, but he was uncommunicative. My friend attempted for some time to explore various options for being of assistance but could not seem to find any resolution. Finally, we concluded that nothing could be done at that time, and we waved good-bye and continued down the street.
>
> Although we didn't end up being able to help, I have often thought with admiration about the charity of my friend.

The man in this story gained a new perspective from watching his friend seek to help a special-needs child. In a miraculous way, the gospel of Jesus Christ also provides a new way of looking at things, one that has enduring consequences. King Benjamin warned us not to circumvent the beggar, not to withhold our assistance and compassion under any circumstances. "For behold, are we not all beggars?" he asked. "Do we not all depend upon the same Being, even God, for all the substance which we have . . . ?" (Mosiah 4:19). So powerful was the king's masterful discourse—based on angelic instruction—that his listeners collapsed under the burden of their own nothingness, perceiving themselves as "even less than the dust of the earth" (Mosiah 4:2). It was only in this state of understanding—this new way of looking at things—that they could admit utter dependence upon the Lord, through whose redeeming merits and mercy alone we can experience the joy of redemption.

In a similar way, are we not all "mortally challenged"— consigned to a state of nothingness because of the fall of mankind into the temporal state? In our present condition, only a mighty change of heart can impart to us "great views of that which is to come" (Mosiah 5:3). Once we perceive our nothingness—"which thing I had never supposed" was the way Moses characterized this traumatic insight (Moses 1:10)—then the Spirit can lift our sight to a crystal clear vision of the pathway to salvation involving the wondrous resolution of our challenged condition through the "merits, and mercy, and grace of the Holy Messiah" (2 Nephi 2:8). "Wherefore, all mankind were in a lost and in a fallen state, and ever would be save they should rely on this Redeemer" (1 Nephi 10:6).

Consequently, when we see a beggar or a challenged person, we should see ourselves, and, in this perspective, we should also see our pathway home. That is the pathway of service, obedience, charity, faith, hope, diligence, compassion, humility, even a broken heart and a contrite spirit—the "mighty change" (Mosiah 5:2) of which King Benjamin spoke millennia ago, echoing and confirming the words of all of God's prophets across time.

Only charity—true love of our fellow beings—will overcome selfishness. In the well-known words of Mormon, as quoted by his son Moroni at the close of the Book of Mormon:

> Charity is the pure love of Christ, and it endureth forever; and whoso is found possessed of it at the last day, it shall be well with him.
>
> Wherefore, my beloved brethren, pray unto the Father with all the energy of heart, that ye may be filled with this love, which he hath bestowed upon all who are true followers of his Son, Jesus Christ; that ye may become the sons of God; that when he shall appear we shall be like him, for we shall see him as he is; that we may have this hope; that we may be purified even as he is pure. Amen. (Moroni 7:47–48)

CHAPTER TWELVE
OVERCOMING CONTENTION

*Peace I leave with you, my peace I give unto
you: not as the world giveth, give I unto you. Let not your
heart be troubled, neither let it be afraid.*
—John 14:27

Contention is born of pride and selfishness. The devil is the father of contention, for he seeks to stir up the hearts of men to contend with anger one with another (see 3 Nephi 11:29). Satan rejoices when he can convince people to fight and quarrel, to engage in strife and controversy, to seek their own will in always being right, or to believe that their own way is the best and only way. When Satan has his way, heated debates rage, anger is expressed, the Spirit is lost, and we are left to ourselves as carnal men and women. When contention ripens into iniquity and wickedness, the result is war—a war of words, a war of wills, and eventually, as shown in the Book of Mormon, even a war of bloodshed where the lives of Heavenly Father's children are lost. It all begins with contention. Contention destroys marriages and families every day. It is impossible to feel good when there is contention. The waters of life become too murky to see the good when contention abounds. Only as we come unto Christ fully and seek to possess the love of God can we ever overcome contention and live after the manner of peace and happiness (see 2 Nephi 5:27).

How happy are those who seek peace rather than contention. The natural blessing of this love and peace is happiness rather than the horrible feelings that come from being embroiled in contention (see Matthew 5:9). The Lord has commanded us not to contend (see 2 Nephi 26:32), and His words contain a solution to contention. Rather than contend and harbor ill will toward each other, the scriptures instruct us to have our "hearts knit together in unity and in love one towards another" (Mosiah 18:21).

Prophetic Counsel. Elder Marvin J. Ashton has taught us the following concerning contention:

> Some misunderstand the realm, scope, and dangers of contention. Too many of us are inclined to declare, "Who, me? I am not contentious, and I'll fight anyone who says I am." There are still those among us who would rather lose a friend than an argument. How important it is to know how to disagree without being disagreeable. It behooves all of us to be in the position to involve ourselves in factual discussions and meaningful study, but never in bitter arguments and contention. ("No Time for Contention," *Ensign,* May 1978, 7)

Here are three ideas to consider in ensuring that contention does not detract from the peace and joy of your life:

• **Cultivate a Personal Lifestyle Based on Spiritual Values and Peace.** Pray for peace—for prayer is an absolute in all dimensions of life. Prayer is indispensable as a strategy for dealing with and overcoming contention. You can pray not just for others to understand, but also for you to be understanding and empathetic in any situation, exemplifying the spirit of peace and harmony. You can seek to purify your attitudes and behavior in greater measure so that the Spirit of the Lord can enlighten and direct you in all things (see 2 Nephi 32:5)—especially with the challenge of overcoming contentions and disputations (see 3 Nephi 11:28). Above all, you can be forgiving (see D&C 64:10), for forgiveness is the way of the Lord.

In all of this, you can feast upon the word of God, for it has great power to bring about positive change (see Alma 31:5). Pondering and learning the word of God can transform your heart (see Alma 4:19; Mosiah 28:1–2). As you live by every word that proceeds forth from the mouth of God (see D&C 84:43–45), you will find that it will direct you in all things (see 2 Nephi 32:3). Thus, you can hold to the iron rod (the word of God) so that you and your loved ones might stay on the strait and narrow path and partake of the fruit (the love of God) from the tree of life. As you study the scriptures and pray with all the energy of your heart (see Moroni 7:48), you can literally come unto the Lord and receive and possess the pure love of Christ—charity (see Moroni 7:44–45). You will then be able to promote peace in greater measure in all that you do. Pride and selfishness will have no place in your life. Through humility, you will cultivate a personal relationship with God and recognize your dependence upon Him. The harvest of humility is grand: being submissive (see Mosiah 3:19), easily entreated (see Alma 7:23), teachable, and bringing before God the sacrifice of a broken heart and a contrite spirit (see 3 Nephi 9:20). The blessings that come to those of humble disposition include self-control, the bridling of passions (see Alma 38:12), peaceful discourse (see Psalm 39:1), soft answers (see Proverbs 15:1), and, above all, patience and forbearance (see Matthew 5:38–42; Colossians 3:12–14; D&C 31:9).

• **Become a Peacemaker in Your Relationships with Others.** In all your relationships, you can be positive, not seeking to find fault, lay blame, or criticize, but rather becoming solution oriented. You can face problems with a "How can we solve this together?" attitude rather than asking who is at fault and must be held accountable and even punished. You can seek to be a person of empathy, and the key to this is to listen, listen, listen. Once people feel that they are truly understood, they feel appreciated and of worth. Their ego or strong feelings concerning the matter are moderated so that they can communicate without being defensive or demanding. When those in your circle feel like they are understood, it will be easier to establish and cultivate agreed-upon values, values that bring unity to the group and understanding for the cause that you are involved with—especially in marriage and family activities. We are all to seek unity, for if we are one we are the Lord's (see D&C 38:27). Adversarial relationships can strategically be rooted out with the guidance of the Spirit. There is then no need to argue, retaliate, strongly debate (just to be "right"), or seek vengeance due to pride and selfishness. Confrontation from others can be handled with decency and civility. Situations of contention can be turned into situations of cooperation and collaboration.

Open and honest communication will help to avoid contention. You can discuss things peaceably. Sometimes you might at first have to agree to disagree in regard to an idea, process, or solution to a problem. Time is often an ally in communication. You can be an example of patience in communicating, for sometimes it simply takes time for divergent opinions to coalesce and for a meeting of minds to occur. Remember that the way you say it can make all the difference in your discussions.

• **Focus Daily on the Marvelous Benefits of Cooperation and Unity.** What joy flows from unity, peace, and cooperative enterprise—at home, in the Church, in the work place, and in the community. How can we focus our efforts on achieving such unity? Write things down—at work, at school, and in the marriage and family—that is, make a list of all the good things that are happening. Write down the things you enjoy and the things others do that you appreciate. Your spouse, your children, and your coworkers will love it. Look for the good in others. Praise them with a thank-you note or reminder of their goodness. Your kindness and thoughtfulness will radiate as a beacon of light, and the spirit of contention, if present, will dissipate. Remember that all good things take time—so don't give up. Your patience and kindness will be a crowning blessing in your life and that of your loved ones and friends.

Remind yourself always to be a peacemaker by surrounding yourself with little reminders, prompts, emblems, and gentle prods toward peacemaking (notes, posters, pictures, pins, banners, and requests for input from others). Changing your environment in worthy ways can often change your thought patterns and thus your actions.

The stakes are high: contention can destroy the soul because it is based on pride and selfishness, the devil's destructive tools. It prevents the Holy Spirit from blessing our lives. The power of the Spirit is the key to doing the Lord's will and receiving the revelations and blessings of the Lord in our lives. We should seek the love of God, this precious fruit of the tree of life that can truly help us be a happy people, with no contention in all the land (see 4 Nephi 1:15–16). This love of God is not only the essence of our eternal life—it is also the motivating power to do good and to be good in the here and now. Let us seek always to partake of this fruit, enjoying the blessings of a spiritual life, avoiding contention like the plague, and remembering Christ's words: "Blessed are the peacemakers: for they shall be called the children of God" (Matthew 5:9). One thing is certain about peacemakers—they feel good, even when things seem bad.

Chapter Thirteen
Overcoming Sin

*Yea, this light had infused such joy into
his soul, the cloud of darkness having been dispelled, and
that the light of everlasting life was lit up in his soul, yea, he knew
that this had overcome his natural frame, and he was
carried away in God.*
—Alma 19:6

There is no way we can feel good in sin. There is *no way* we can feel good in sin. Oh, we may have momentary pleasure—but the ensuing hours bring nothing but sorrow, misery, and lamenting of the past. Alma described his sorrow for sin and his subsequent joy through repentance and forgiveness. The horror of his initial state comes through his words with clarity: "The very thought of coming into the presence of my God did rack my soul with inexpressible horror." And moreover, "Oh, thought I, that I could be banished and become extinct both soul and body. . . . I say unto you . . . that there could be nothing so exquisite and so bitter as were my pains." Then the miracle happened through the process of repentance and forgiveness: "I could remember my pains no more; yea, I was harrowed up by the memory of my sins no more. And oh, what joy, and what marvelous light I did behold; yea, my soul was filled with joy as exceeding as was my pain! . . . Yea, and again I say unto you . . . there can be nothing so exquisite and sweet as was my joy" (Alma 36:14–21).

Understanding Sin. A willfully unrighteous thought or

action—or the lack of an action required for the keeping of righteous principles—is considered a sin. It is transgressing the law of God (see 1 John 3:4). When we sin, we withdraw ourselves from the Spirit (see Mosiah 2:36) and become more easily influenced by the devil and his temptations (see D&C 29:40) because the devil "inviteth and enticeth to sin" (Moroni 7:12). All people have sinned (see 1 John 1:8–10)—but we are free to choose righteousness rather than sin (see 2 Nephi 2:27). The test of life is to make good choices and to repent of our sins by exercising faith unto repentance (see Alma 34:15–17). The Lord makes no allowance for sin, but He is compassionate and merciful to the repentant sinner (see D&C 1:31–32)—for we cannot be saved in our sins (see Alma 11:37). When we confess and forsake our sins, the Lord remembers them no more, and we obtain forgiveness (see D&C 58:42–43).

President Kimball taught these great truths about sin:

> The attractiveness of sin is a lie. Have you seen a real mirage in the distance with lakes and trees and dwellings and castles and water, but as the thirsty traveler moves on and on and on through it, he finds it but an illusion, and when he has gone too far to return he stumbles choking in the desert deception. That is like life—wealth and pride, wit and physical charm, popularity and flattery are the shadows of the nothingness that can bring us only disappointment and frustration. . . . Sin is slavery. . . . Sin limits progress. Since the beginning there has been in the world a wide range of sins. Many of them involve harm to others, but every sin is against ourselves and God, for sins limit our progress, curtail our development, and estrange us from good people, good influences, and from our Lord. (*The Teachings of Spencer W. Kimball* [Salt Lake City: Bookcraft, 1982], 153)

When we succumb to sin, we subject ourselves to the consequences of the sin according to the natural law that applies—we lose the Spirit (see Mosiah 2:36), and then we lose all the blessings associated with keeping the commandment. Let us remember that all good comes from God and that all evil and sin are of the devil, for he is the "author of all sin" (Helaman 6:30).

Understanding Repentance and Forgiveness. The Atonement of Jesus Christ makes possible the miracle of repentance and forgiveness. Repentance is the process of becoming clean from sin. Through faith on Jesus Christ we can be forgiven and our guilt can be swept away (see Enos 1:6–8). Faith and repentance are preached continually throughout all the scriptures and by our living prophets today. Repentance is necessary to our salvation (see D&C 20:29). Repentance and baptism are the gateway into the kingdom of God and a prerequisite for entrance into the celestial kingdom (see D&C 20:71). All must repent, for all have sinned (see 1 John 1:8), and if we do not repent, we must suffer even as our Savior Jesus Christ (see D&C 19:15–19).

Our salvation, immortality, and eternal life depend on us overcoming and forsaking sins. We are to repent—there is no other way back into the presence of our Heavenly Father. The process of repentance through the Atonement of our Savior is a wonderful gift—yet how much less painful it is to make righteous choices and learn from the scriptures and our leaders than to learn everything on the earth by trial and error. Alma said it correctly when he said, "O, remember, my son, and learn wisdom in thy youth; yea, learn in thy youth to keep the commandments of God" (Alma 37:35). The Prophet Jacob similarly counseled in regard to repentance and staying on the straight and narrow path, "O be wise; what can I say more?" (Jacob 6:12).

Lehi taught that "by the law no flesh is justified" (2 Nephi 2:5)—meaning that no mortal can perfectly live every aspect of the law of God—hence the need for a Savior. Through His perfect sacrifice, Jesus Christ extended the arms of mercy unto all who repent and come to Him in faith and humility with a broken heart and a contrite spirit. Said Nephi, "For we labor diligently to write, to persuade our children, and also our brethren, to believe in Christ, and to be reconciled to God; for we know that it is by grace that we are saved, after all we can do" (2 Nephi 25:23). Perfection is therefore not so much in living a perfect life as it is in living a life of perfect repentance. Through the grace of God, we can be perfected in Christ (see Moroni 10:32).

The Lord invites all of us to seek justification and sanctification through the Atonement and the blessing of the Holy Ghost. We are to be cleansed from iniquity and thus enabled to perform miracles (see 3 Nephi 8:1). Surely repentance is the single greatest thing we can do in regard to our individual salvation. We can feel good as we repent and become clean through the goodness of God and the infinite and eternal Atonement.

Prophetic Counsel. Repentance is a process, not an event, and healing takes time. As President Harold B. Lee explained, "*We must repent daily.* In order for good to blossom it must be cultivated and exercised by constant practice, and to be truly righteous there is required a daily pruning of the evil growth of our characters by a daily repentance from sin" (*The Teachings of Harold B. Lee,* ed. Clyde J. Williams [Salt Lake City: Bookcraft, 1996], 113).

Since continual repentance is truly necessary for us to feel good and enjoy the blessings of the Lord, let's review the steps of the process:

- **Recognize your sin.** Become aware of your sin to the point that you realize you should repent.
- **Feel godly sorrow for sin.** Recognition that you have sinned should lead you to feel godly sorrow, having a broken

heart and a contrite spirit, which "worketh repentance to salvation" (2 Corinthians 7:10). Godly sorrow is motivated by love of God, not social pressures. A broken heart and contrite spirit are the offering we give the Lord as a sacrifice before Him (see 3 Nephi 9:20).

- **Forsake the sin.** Once you feel godly sorrow for your sin, you should stop committing the sin and forsake it completely (see D&C 58:42–43).

- **Confess the sin.** True repentance includes confessing your sins to Heavenly Father and, when necessary, to your bishop (see D&C 64:7). "Without sincere confession of sin repentance is impossible," said James E. Talmage (*The Vitality of Mormonism* [Salt Lake City: Deseret Book, 1919], 83).

- **Make restitution for the sin.** Where possible, you should restore that which was taken or destroyed by your sin. We often cannot make full restitution due to the nature of the sin, but the power of the Atonement compensates for our inadequacies in making restitution (see Alma 7:11–12).

- **Forgive others.** In order to receive forgiveness for your sins, you must forgive others of their sins, "for he that forgiveth not his brother his trespasses standeth condemned before the Lord; for there remaineth in him the greater sin" (D&C 64:9).

- **Make a commitment not to sin again.** In order to seal your repentance, you must make a commitment to not sin again but to be obedient to all the commandments and endure to the end in righteousness (see 2 Nephi 31:19–21).

The Transforming Power of Repentance. A bishop recalls an event during his tenure that illustrates the transforming power of repentance:

> Here was a delightful young couple preparing for marriage—bright, faithful in Church participation, eager to do the right thing. But

now there was a problem—a compromising of values and propriety. They were embarrassed and heartbroken as they sat across from me, wondering what to do about their sin. We counseled. We sorrowed together. We pondered the consequences. But we also took comfort together in the process of repentance empowered by the Atonement. Yes, there needed to be change. There needed to be prayerful godly sorrow and faithful commitment to a better lifestyle. But they had caught themselves at the edge of the precipice, they had recoiled under the strength of conscience, and they now wanted to do right before the Lord. They were good young people with the desire for righteousness. The Lord loved them and wanted them to have the fulness of His blessings. There needed to be some regular appointments for a few weeks to give momentum to the new commitments, but things went very well. They rebounded. They prospered. Their faces glowed with the light of peace once again. They rose to new heights, and once more the age-old story of the gospel transforming lives was repeated in a real-life setting. Thank heavens for the principles of the gospel. Thank heavens for the Atonement of Jesus Christ.

The Lord has made it clear that in order for us to apply and live the gospel of Jesus Christ we are to repent and come unto Him (see 3 Nephi 27:20–21). Repentance is the key to exaltation, and the time to repent is now (see Alma 34:31–35). We can be saved through the Atonement and grace of God "after all we can do" (2 Nephi 25:23). We can scarcely be perfect on our own, but we can be "perfect in Christ" (Moroni 10:33) because perfection comes through the grace of God and our willingness to repent perfectly. Let us therefore choose to repent and become clean and free from sin. There are unspeakable blessings that await the repentant soul who is valiant in the quest to endure to the end in faith and obedience. There is no joy in sin, and wickedness never was and never will be happiness (see Alma 41:10), but through repentance we can taste the joy of being forgiven, and the Spirit will bring peace and love to our lives.

CHAPTER FOURTEEN
OVERCOMING BLAME

I, the Lord, will forgive whom I will forgive, but
of you it is required to forgive all men.
—*D&C 64:10*

When we stop and think about life and our personal responsibilities, things could be summarized in two words—repent and forgive. Our happiness and capacity to feel good about life and our fellowmen is often determined by our capacity to forgive. The capacity to forgive is one of the most divine attributes one can possess. It is a commandment of God (see Matthew 6:15). It is a quality that will bring peace to our souls and allow others to find peace as well. True forgiveness is without a doubt the most difficult aspect of all human behavior to practice. It is an expression of godliness.

Let us remember that our own forgiveness is directly tied to our forgiving others—something we are commanded to do (see 3 Nephi 13:14–15). We are forgiven and exalted through the Atonement as we forgive others—such forgiveness is an important aspect of doing "all we can do" to merit the grace of our Lord (2 Nephi 25:23). Forgiveness is tied to our righteousness to such an extent that we are condemned of the Lord—and we have the greater sin—if we fail to forgive others (see D&C 64:9). How can this be so when we are sometimes victims? The Lord was the greatest victim of all and yet He uttered, "Father, forgive them; for they know not what they do" (Luke 23:34). Christ was forgiving by nature. Though the sins of His oppressors were egregious, He forgave them. That is what we must do: forgive. This then makes possible our being forgiven when we repent (see D&C 82:1).

Prophetic Counsel. Concerning the commandment to forgive others, President Spencer W. Kimball questioned:

> Do we follow that command or do we sulk in our bitterness, waiting for our offender to learn of it and to kneel to us in remorse?
>
> And this reconciliation suggests also forgetting. Unless you forget, have you forgiven? A woman in a branch in the mission field where there had been friction finally capitulated and said, "Yes, I will forgive the others, but I have an eternal memory." Certainly she had not fulfilled the law of forgiving. She was meeting the letter but not the spirit. Frequently we say we forgive, then permit the grievance to continue to poison and embitter us.
>
> The Lord forgets when He has forgiven, and certainly must we. He inspired Isaiah to say: "I, even I, am he that blotteth out thy transgressions for mine own sake, and will not remember thy sins." (Isaiah 43:25)
>
> No bitterness of past frictions can be held in memory if we forgive with all our hearts. (*Faith Precedes the Miracle* [Salt Lake City: Deseret Book, 1972], 194)

President Kimball also reminded us: "He who will not forgive others breaks down the bridge over which he himself must travel. This is a truth taught by the Lord in the parable of the unmerciful servant who demanded to be forgiven but was merciless to one who asked forgiveness of him. (See Matthew 18:23–35)" (*The Miracle of Forgiveness* [Salt Lake City: Bookcraft, 1969], 269).

The Prophet Joseph Smith counseled us: "Meekly persuade and urge everyone to forgive one another all their trespasses, offenses and sins, that they may work out their own salvation with fear and trembling. Brethren, bear and forbear one with another, for so the Lord does with us. Pray for your enemies in the Church and curse not your foes without: for vengeance is mine, saith the Lord, and I will repay. To every ordained member, and to all, we say, be merciful and you shall find mercy" (*HC* 2:229–30).

When We Are Wrongly Accused. Many have experienced the feeling of being condemned by others unjustly or accused of unkind motives that they have never harbored. Perhaps you have had that experience yourself. The Prophet Joseph Smith received more than his fair share of false accusation and was even subjected to the most vile derision and persecution without cause or provocation. His response was consistent: he forgave and moved on with undaunted spirit. He fought for the right and defended the Church and its doctrines indefatigably in the face of the most outrageous lies and malicious attacks. He fought valiantly and forcefully, but he forgave, nonetheless.

Consider his behavior toward those who inflicted serious bodily harm upon him one Saturday evening. At that time, he and his family were staying at the home of John Johnson in Hiram, Ohio. Suddenly, a mob of some two dozen drunken men tore Joseph from the side of his ailing son, eleven-month-old Joseph Murdock Smith (one of two adopted twins), dragged him from the house, stripped him of his clothes, beat him brutally, and tarred and feathered him. All during that night friends and family removed the skin-searing tar from his body, taking up large areas of skin in the process. Young Joseph Murdock Smith, already suffering with measles, contracted pneumonia from the exposure that night and was to die a few days later. And yet, on Sunday morning, the day after the brutal attack, Joseph delivered a sermon before the gathering of Saints. Also in the congregation that day were a number of the mob from the night before. Joseph did not take the opportunity to call out his attackers. In rising that morning to preach the gospel as usual, he demonstrated to the gathered Saints a resolve to forge ahead, to not seek revenge but to exemplify the peace of the gospel of Christ. A number of individuals were baptized that afternoon (see *HC* 1:261–265).

It was an instance of forgiveness and a reminder of the Prophet's understanding of the Lord's injunction to cultivate a forgiving heart and practice forgiveness every day: "Ye have heard that it hath been said, Thou shalt love thy neighbor, and hate thine enemy. But I say unto you, Love your enemies, bless them that curse you, do good to them that hate you, and pray for them which despitefully use you, and persecute you; That ye may be the children of your Father which is in heaven . . ." (Matthew 5:43–45).

As you strive to master the principle of forgiveness, here are some ideas that might be helpful:

- **Forgiveness is not just something you *do*—it is something you *are*.** Forgiveness shows the quality of a Christlike character, revealing the process of becoming even as He is (see 3 Nephi 27:27). The forgiving person has made the pure love of Christ the foundation of his or her life, forgiveness being a sure sign of that love. Thus, forgiveness is a sign of true strength, based on empathy and understanding.
- **Forgiveness brings a host of values and benefits in its wake.** Below are listed some of the myriad benefits of forgiveness.
  - **Peace**—You will have more peace if you forgive.
  - **Liberty**—Forgiveness frees you of hurt, anger, and the desire to retaliate and seek vengeance.
  - **Productivity**—Forgiveness increases your ability to be creative and productive, whereas a grudging disposition saps creativity and draws you into a non-productive downward spiral.

- **Self-confidence**—Forgive yourself by learning from your own mistakes and going on with life; it will increase your understanding of others and enhance your wisdom.
- **Unity**—Forgiveness helps heal relationships and restore unity.
- **Forgiveness is a divine process that works.** It simply makes good sense to be forgiving because it helps you to come to know your true nature better. By forgiving others, you come to understand that everyone makes mistakes—even you. When a perceived offense occurs, you can clarify the matter with the "offending" party, often discovering that there was simply a misunderstanding with no intention of giving offense. Communication is priceless in maintaining unity and amity. At the same time, you know that forgiving others in the wake of a genuine offense doesn't give absolution for the perpetrator. That person is ultimately responsible for his or her own actions and will need to make peace with God for them. When a person has been forgiven for an offense, it does not mean that he or she will altogether forget but rather that he or she will find peace and freedom from guilt through the principle of repentance and the blessing of the Lord. The real trick isn't to forget the past, but to learn from the past and try to use the added wisdom to help others both now and in the future.

It is clear that God's children are expected to unconditionally forgive. As one considers the act of forgiveness, remember that mercy begets mercy. The duty of the offender is to change and repent, but we are all required to forgive. There is no question of the freedom and peace one receives when forgiving others. Forgiveness is truly a quality of godliness and one of the defining characteristics of the children of God. Through forgiveness, we can feel good, even when things seem bad.

CHAPTER FIFTEEN
OVERCOMING DEBT

*That through my providence, notwithstanding
the tribulation which shall descend upon you, that the church
may stand independent above all other creatures
beneath the celestial world.*
—*D&C 78:14*

Debt can make you a prisoner in your own life. Interest accruing from your debts never sleeps—it just keeps adding up. We have all faced debt in our lives and know it can be our enemy. We should avoid debt, except for those major purchases that are financially sound and designed to be paid off in an appropriate and systematic manner. At the same time, we should be reasonable and compassionate toward those who are indebted to us and help them systematically move toward financial independence.

Let us maintain our focus on things of eternity rather than on things of a material nature. Let us be liberated from the clutches of Babylon. Let us remember the words of the Lord: "Seek not for riches but for wisdom, and behold, the mysteries of God shall be unfolded unto you, and then shall you be made rich. Behold, he that hath eternal life is rich" (D&C 6:7). Independence and self-reliance are moral imperatives to live by (see D&C 58:27–28; 78:14). Freedom from temporal indebtedness permits greater views of spiritual matters and greater loyalty to the giver of all blessings and endowments.

Prophetic Counsel. Elder L. Tom Perry gave this advice about debt and interest: "It is so easy to allow consumer debt to get out of hand. If you do not have the discipline to control the use of credit cards, it is better not to have them. A well-managed family does not pay interest—it earns it. The definition I received from a wise boss at one time in my early business career was 'Thems that understands interest receives it, thems that don't pays it'" ("If Ye Are Prepared Ye Shall Not Fear," *Ensign,* Nov. 1995, 35).

The following are three ideas to help manage or eliminate debt:

- **Take care of first things first.** As soon as you receive your income, follow the 10/10 rule: First, pay 10 percent tithing and a generous fast offering, plus contribute to other Church-related funds or other worthy causes. Next, pay another 10 percent to yourself (savings)—then live off the rest. Let the miracle of compound interest help secure your future (*your* interest income, not *theirs*). Remember to give of yourself: Instead of spending more money *on* the family, spend more time *with* the family. You can't buy love, but you can give it away and create far more harmony, balance, peace, and happiness than money can buy.
- **Budget according to solid principles.** Those who want to triumph over debt strive to be realistic in budgeting by tracking expenses to discover the areas of expenditure that could be reduced. Practicing self-mastery is the key—living *within* our means. So many of us find ways to live beyond our means, to spend it all, and even more than our income. The key is to accommodate needs but discipline wants— wants being defined as nice but unnecessary options and needs being defined as instruments of actual survival. We can avoid debt in the first place—except for major purchases such as a home, an automobile, or other significant items that are essential and within our means. A measure of wisdom is to avoid spending what we don't have and to stay clear of obligating ourselves for debt with money we have not earned and will not likely earn.

In that context, all of us should beware of fixed debt that requires too great a percentage of our fixed income. If we experience a job loss or decreased earnings, our capacity to handle our debt could be curtailed or eliminated. In that context, we can undergo "plastic surgery"—quarantining our credit cards except when we are required to pay with a secured arrangement (such as for hotels or rental cars).

Overall, you can become an expert at self-control, being discount- and best-deal conscious, carrying sufficient insurance, maintaining cars and equipment meticulously, insulating your home for added savings on utilities, eating a wholesome diet, investing wisely, and being creative—such as having a family vegetable garden and fruit trees where possible (even apartments can have potted tomato plants). With a sense of creativity, you and family members can also turn hobbies into cash where possible.

- **Take the lead in family financing.** You can organize a family financial team, even letting the older children increase their financial skills by contributing to family upkeep. You can match their savings as they save for specific purchases, such as sports equipment and travel excursions. Set the example by systematically eliminating family debt. One approach is to calculate how much extra per month your family would have to pay in order to be debt-free within a reasonable time (five or ten years, say). For a typical family this may not be more than a few hundred dollars per month, including mortgages. Then the family can set a goal to come up with the redeeming dollar amount through coordinated belt-tightening, careful budgeting, and even additional streams of income. The highest interest debts are paid off first. After the debt is all paid off, the extra monthly amount can be shifted into savings or wise investments. That's it! Meanwhile, teach family members how to build for the future by starting a savings account for each child or grandchild, discussing it with them, encouraging them to contribute to it, and having them watch it grow as they grow. Teach others to find happiness in the moment—the kind of happiness that is not to be found in exotic getaway locations, in surpassing the Joneses, or in having more of this or that than you ever dreamed of—but rather the kind of happiness that is found in family unity and harmony, peace of soul, joy in living, and the spiritual well-being that comes from covenant valor in the kingdom of God.

Financial Questions to Ponder. In your efforts to avoid or eliminate debt, consider the following questions with your spouse:

- What determines our authentic value: what we *have* or who we *are?*
- Do we tend to protect our children from the normal adversities and challenges of life by giving them more and more in the way of temporal things? How can we come to understand that moderating our amount of giving to our children might indeed show more love for them than an overabundance of generosity?
- How do we protect our family from the infectious philosophy of "entitlement" promulgated so often in the media? How do we instead teach our children self-reliance, self-confidence, and the ability to develop their talents and cultivate true initiative?
- What standard of living is in alignment with our income stream? How do we bring the two into harmony?
- Are we prepared for unexpected emergencies?

These and similar questions are raised and treated wisely by financial advisor Bernard Poduska in his article "Debt Doesn't Have to Be Forever" (Ensign, Jan. 2001, 59). His counsel concludes with these words:

> As we take into consideration some of the underlying reasons that might be contributing to chronic debt, we can begin a process that,

with faith and prayer, can help us make better choices. If we pray to know the truth and to see clearly our needs and how best to meet them, we can receive spiritual guidance in handling our temporal affairs. Then, when we come to know and acknowledge the truth about ourselves, our motives, and our unmet needs, we can free ourselves of unproductive behavior and move toward living within our incomes.

Let us remember that each of us can learn to deal with debt and discover practical solutions for freeing ourselves from its insidious tentacles. Let us be frugal and wise. Let us organize well our financial lives and learn to live within our means. Life is far more enjoyable when we are debt-free rather than in bondage to creditors. By managing our habits, planning wisely, and exerting self-discipline, we can become debt-free. Let us place our focus on spiritual matters and remove ourselves from the entanglements of materialism and unnecessary debt. Let us manage our personal and family matters according to the counsel the Lord laid down for progress within His kingdom: "That through my providence, notwithstanding the tribulation which shall descend upon you, that the church may stand independent above all other creatures beneath the celestial world; That you may come up unto the crown prepared for you, and be made rulers over many kingdoms, saith the Lord God, the Holy One of Zion" (D&C 78:14–15).

CHAPTER SIXTEEN
COPING WITH STRESS

*And see that all these things are done
in wisdom and order; for it is not requisite that a
man should run faster than he has strength. And again,
it is expedient that he should be diligent, that thereby
he might win the prize; therefore, all things must
be done in order.*
—Mosiah 4:27

Dealing with life's pressures often creates stress. Stress is the feeling that puts pressure on us to the point that we worry, we're full of anxiety, we feel overwhelmed, and sometimes we literally feel physically ill. Each person responds differently to demands; what causes stress for one is often not stressful for another.

Prophetic Counsel. What can we do to avoid "stressing out" to the point that our productivity suffers and we slacken our duties to family, church, and society? Elder Neal A. Maxwell gave this advice:

> The stress most faithful Church members feel arises out of the shared pressures of daily life, the temptations and afflictions common to mortals. These real pressures are unnecessarily increased when some unwisely place upon themselves unrealistic expectations. As to this avoidable stress, the Lord's instructions are very clear:

"Do not run faster or labor more than you have strength and means provided. . . ." (D&C 10:4). . . .

While we cannot expect discipleship to be cost free, we can receive God's helping grace, including compensatory blessings, along with inner joy over what is jettisoned in putting off the natural man. Thereby we can, for instance, end the gnawing stress of being unsettled: "Wherefore, settle this in your hearts, that ye will do the things which I shall teach, and command you" (JST, Luke 14:28). . . .

We can also end the genuine stress which goes with unrepented-of sin by pleading, "More holiness give me," and by receiving the "peace . . . which passeth all understanding" (*Hymns*, no. 131; John 14:27; Philippians 4:7). . . .

We can dissolve the stress of wearily listening to "so many kinds of voices in the world" (1 Corinthians 14:10). A true disciple need tune in on only one channel: "My sheep hear my voice" (John 10:27). (*Men and Women of Christ* [Salt Lake City: Bookcraft, 1991], 25–26)

Since stress has become one of the major problems of our high-intensity culture, it might be well to consider a few ideas about stress that may help you deal with it effectively:

- **Stress has its positive elements.** Stress is, in a way, part of the normal stream of life, since it contributes to forward motion in maintaining relationships, upward progress, reputation, honor, and character. All of this is a life-supporting kind of stress that can be productive. Ironically, stress is often needed to galvanize one to positive action, leading to relief of the conditions that caused the stress in the first place. Stress is also a survival factor—in athletics or in any time where there is a physical threat that activates the "fight or flight" mechanism—stress is vital for generating greater effort in our physical capacities. When you understand this, you can recognize that stress has a positive influence—as long as you can manage it and transform it into a catalyst for productive outcomes.

• **You need to get the facts before you act.** Positive action depends on being informed. Better understanding of the stressful situation and its ramifications will help you choose an appropriate attitude and behavior. You can look at the root causes to be sure there are no physiological problems promoting a stress response—anxiety disorder, mood swings, chemical imbalance, etc. If such problems do exist, it is wise to seek professional help in addition to applying the other elements of relief outlined here.

• **You can often dispel stress just by the way you think.** Rethinking goals and analyzing the source of stress can lead to a fundamental change of strategy: If the stress is resulting from an obsession with unimportant goals or fads—keeping up with the Joneses, the pursuit of material things devoid of lasting value, fleeting fashions—then a change of direction can reduce stress and promote balance, harmony, and peace in your life. In effect, you can clean house, getting rid of the sacred cows that are not so sacred: false formulas such as "I can never make a mistake or people won't respect me," "I must be perfect," or "I am inadequate." Even amid the stress of the everyday world, you can change your inner thoughts to positive, self-fulfilling prophecies such as "I will find a way," "I will get better at this with practice," and "I will get through this with flying colors." Similarly, you can divest yourself of superstitious shackles, such as a belief in "bad luck," and recognize all worthwhile objectives are attainable, through devoted initiative and in the strength of the Lord.

• **You can dilute unavoidable stress.** Some things are beyond our control. Stress over things you cannot change can be offset by seeking balance in your life, integrating into the flow of activities ample opportunity for relaxation, exercise, recreation, and peace-generating time-outs. You can practice relaxation techniques. You can allow yourself to sit in your favorite chair for a few minutes, breathing deeply and imagining that you are relaxing in your favorite place. There are wholesome outcomes from doing such things as needed.

• **You can get help from others.** You can organize a "stress team" to help you manage the burdens that weigh down on you. The support of others is a comforting feeling that will give you strength in knowing that you are not alone. In effect, you can delegate stress by spreading it out in effective ways. Remember how overtaxed Moses was as the chief judge in Israel until his father-in-law, Jethro, gave him an inspired lesson in delegation (see Exodus 18:13–27). Similarly, you can learn from the experts, asking people you admire how they deal with stress and then adopting a few of their strategies.

• **Purposeful action dispels stress.** The greatest antidote to stress is a planned, daily schedule of little key actions that can leverage your success toward the attainment of meaningful goals. By dividing the big goals into smaller, manageable ones, you can minimize stress and move forward systematically. The traditional wisdom has it that we should "hope for the best and prepare for the worst." In that context, practice makes perfect—it also decreases stress. Whether you are giving presentations, talks, or major performances, the more you do it the less stress you'll encounter. If your stress relates to things that you cannot control—the weather, your place of birth, your height or genes, for example—then convert the "worry energy" into actions that overcome or compensate for what you perceive as a challenge.

• **You can deploy key stress-reducing strategies.** Preparation, knowledge, and experience will decrease the stress you encounter. They will give you power and confidence to control your environment, layer your time in skillful ways to accomplish multiple objectives simultaneously (shopping with the family, thinking creatively while doing chores, and learning while serving), and eliminate time-wasters in your life (such as excessive TV viewing) and replace them with more productive tasks. They will also enable you to keep systematic tabs on your progress to confirm that your deadlines will be met according to plans.

- **You can find peace in God.** Peace comes only through true repentance as we come unto Christ with full purpose of heart. Practice true discipleship by keeping the commandments, searching the scriptures, fasting and praying, honoring the priesthood, and magnifying your callings. When you are at peace with the Lord, you will be at peace with yourself. Life's trials and stress-producing moments will be easier to handle.

If all of this feels a bit overwhelming, you can remember that time is your ally—sooner or later things will get better. You can also remember to do things in order, here a little and there a little, as seems appropriate.

Stress is part of life. Pressure is part of the mortal journey. We can learn to deal with the ups and downs of life by keeping things in focus, balancing our efforts in wisdom, and following the guidance of the Spirit. That way we can endure to the end in courage—and learn to feel good, even when things seem bad.

CHAPTER SEVENTEEN
COPING WITH DISAPPOINTMENT

*And the members shall manifest before the
church, and also before the elders, by a godly walk and
conversation, that they are worthy of it, that there may be
works and faith agreeable to the holy scriptures—
walking in holiness before the Lord.*
—D&C 20:69

When things don't go our way we can feel disappointed.
The range of emotions can be quite broad, but the
good news is this: being disappointed doesn't have to last
forever. In fact, we can learn to bounce back and feel better
once we can see things more clearly—thus reminding
ourselves of the blessing that comes with the passage of time.
Time gives us a better perspective and often heals the ups
and downs of life.

The causes of disappointment range from the most minor
happenings to major letdowns in important areas of our
lives. But no matter how severe the dilemma, the same
principles are used to solve it. We can learn to walk in faith
and holiness before the Lord—and know that with His help
our disappointments will fade as feathers in the wind.

Prophetic Counsel. President Gordon B. Hinckley gives
us insight into disappointment and how to deal with it:

> There is something of a tendency among us
> to think that everything must be lovely and

rosy and beautiful without realizing that even adversity has some sweet uses. . . .

We may know much of loneliness. We may know discouragement and frustration. We may know adversity and trouble and pain. I would hope not. But you know, and I know, that suffering comes to many. Sometimes it is mental. Sometimes it is physical. Sometimes it may even be spiritual. Ours is the duty to walk by faith.

Ours is the duty to walk in faith, rising above the evils of the world. We are sons and daughters of God. Ours is a divine birthright. Ours is a divine destiny. We must not, we cannot sink to the evils of the world—to selfishness and sin, to hate and envy and backbiting, to the "mean and beggarly" elements of life.

You and I must walk on a higher plane. It may not be easy, but we can do it. Our great example is the Son of God whom we wish to follow. (*Teachings of Gordon B. Hinckley* [Salt Lake City: Deseret Book, 1997], 6–7)

In this spirit of hope and conviction, there are things you can consider doing to feel better in times of disappointment:

- **Remember that everyone has disappointments in life.** The rain falls on the just and the unjust (see Matthew 5:45), and everyone faces trials and disappointments. Keep in mind that without some disappointments you could never appreciate the good times. Disappointments can also lead to change for the better. They can cause you to re-evaluate your values, goals, and plans—and put in place initiatives that will lead to greater blessings. Most importantly, disappointments can cause you to draw closer to the Lord.
- **Apply principles and ideas to deal with disappointment.** The gospel of Jesus Christ offers an abundance of principles

and ideas for dealing with disappointment. Prayer can unfold avenues of resolution and adjustment for the better (see James 1:5–6; Mosiah 27:14; Alma 13:28; 34:17–28; D&C 4:7). The word of God can open to your mind and heart possibilities and promises for overcoming disappointment (see 2 Nephi 32:3) and the ability to bring about positive change (see Alma 31:5). The Holy Ghost can bring into view things you can do for greater happiness and joy (see 2 Nephi 32:5) as you experience the comforting influence of the Spirit (see John 14:16, 26). You can do all things by faith (see Moroni 7:33; 10:23). Through hope all things can work together for your good (see D&C 122:7). Your leaders and trusted friends can support you in your hour of need (see Mosiah 18:8–9; D&C 81:5; 108:7). You have the power to choose your response in every circumstance.

• **Look for the benefits that come from adversity and disappointment.** When you realize that everything in life is a test and an opportunity for growth, you can look for the benefits that come from adversity and disappointment. Disappointments can bring humility. Disappointments can help you turn to the Lord. Overcoming the disappointments of life will help you get through other trials in the future with courage and fortitude. You may even be able to help others as they face similar disappointments.

There is wisdom in not being overwhelmed by disappointments but rather meeting them head-on with a conscious awareness that they are essential for our growth. In that way we can handle difficulties on a more even keel. When our emotions run rampant, our ability to handle stressful situations diminishes. At times of disappointment, we can take a deep breath, step back strategically, and study out the situation causing the disappointment. In this methodical approach we can be more objective, strengthening our resolve to move forward in quest of viable solutions leading to greater joy and happiness. We can indeed come to feel good, even when things seem bad.

CHAPTER EIGHTEEN
COPING WITH WAYWARD CHILDREN

*What man of you, having an hundred
sheep, if he lose one of them, doth not leave the
ninety and nine in the wilderness, and go after that which
is lost, until he find it? And when he hath found it,
he layeth it on his shoulders, rejoicing.*
—*Luke 15:4–5*

Nothing tugs at the heartstrings of a parent more than a struggling, wayward child. It seems as though we become consumed by their behavior and misdeeds. We feel overwhelmed and wonder, "What did I do wrong?" We need to remember that agency is supreme, and everyone has the guidance of the light of Christ. Our hope is in loving the wayward with a perfect love, remembering that they are Heavenly Father's children too, and never giving up. There is much we can do. Note this special counsel for parents from Elder Marvin J. Ashton:

> When I think of the Savior's admonition to do cheerfully all things that lie in our power, I think of the father of the prodigal son. The father was heartbroken by the loss and conduct of his wayward son. Yet we have no mention of his lamenting, "Where did I go wrong?" "What have I done to deserve this?" Or, "Where did I fail?"
>
> Instead he seemed to have endured without bitterness his son's misconduct and welcomed him back with love. "For this my son was dead, and

is alive again; he was lost, and is found. And they began to be merry." (Luke 15:24)

When family members disappoint us, we especially need to learn endurance. As long as we exercise love, patience, and understanding, even when no progress is apparent, we are not failing. We must keep trying. (*Be of Good Cheer* [Salt Lake City: Deseret Book, 1987], 18)

Prophetic Counsel. President Howard W. Hunter said "parents of wayward children should remember eight helpful thoughts":

First, such a father or mother is not alone. Our first parents knew the pain and suffering of seeing some of their children reject the teachings of eternal life (see Moses 5:27). . . . Our Father in Heaven has also lost many of his spirit children to the world; he knows the feelings of your heart.

Second, we should remember that errors of judgment are generally less serious than errors of intent.

Third, even if there was a mistake made with full knowledge and understanding, there is the principle of repentance for release. . . .

Fourth, don't give up hope for a boy or a girl who has strayed. Many who have appeared to be completely lost have returned. We must be prayerful and, if possible, let our children know of our love and concern.

Fifth, remember that ours was not the only influence that contributed to the actions of our children, whether those actions were good or bad.

Sixth, know that our Heavenly Father will recognize the love and the sacrifice, the worry and the concern, even though our great effort has been unsuccessful. . . .

Seventh, whatever the sorrow, whatever the concern, whatever the pain and anguish, look for a way to turn it to beneficial use—perhaps in helping others to avoid the same problems. . . .

The eighth and final point of reminder is that everyone is different. . . . We must not assume that the Lord will judge the success of one in precisely the same way as another. . . . We should be careful in our judgments. (*The Teachings of Howard W. Hunter,* ed. Clyde J. Williams [Salt Lake City: Bookcraft, 1997], 148; compare also Alexander B. Morrison, "Fire Where Once Were Ashes," *Ensign,* Aug. 1990, 7)

Here are some further ideas that might be helpful:

- **Love everyone.** We are commanded to love everyone with the pure love of Christ (see John 13:34–35; John 15:12; 2 Peter 1:7). The pure love of Christ will provide strength and support as we seek to bless those who have strayed (see Moroni 7:48; D&C 4:6). Our mission is to find them and nurture them (see John 21:15–17; Moroni 6:1–4), understand their situation in kind and loving ways (see JST, Matthew 7:1–2), and determine and clarify their needs (see Proverbs 3:4–5).
- **Seek counsel and strength from the Lord and the Spirit.** We are to seek direction from the Lord through prayer (see Jacob 4:10; 2 Nephi 9:29; 3 Nephi 14:7), through revelation and inspiration by the Spirit (see 2 Nephi 32:5), from the scriptures (see 2 Nephi 3:23), and from our leaders (see D&C 108:1). The Lord is always there to help us and strengthen us in all things (see Alma 26:11–12).
- **The wayward need to feel our love.** People don't often care how much we know until they know how much we care. We must be true friends. When love is felt, people are drawn by its magnificent motivating power (see 3 Nephi 27:13–15; John 3:16; 2 Nephi 26:24; Alma 7:11–12).

- **Utilize all the resources available.** There is a grand inventory of resources for helping those who have gone astray: family, friends, ward leaders, ward council, and everything that the Lord inspires us to do. Caution: even though the resources are plentiful, we must proceed in wisdom, at the proper pace, and according to the individual's capacity to change. Remember, this is not a program of efficiency—it is an expression of never-deviating love and concern for the welfare of our brother or sister.

- **Seek to strengthen their faith in Christ.** The most fundamental part of bringing stragglers back to the fold of the gospel is strengthening their faith in Christ. The Savior can become their rock (see Helaman 5:12). This helps them become spiritually self-sufficient. We can "focus on the one" as directed by the Spirit (see 3 Nephi 11:15), committing ourselves never to give up while acting as instruments in the hands of the Lord to bless those struggling Saints who desperately need help. We can press forward with unwearyingness (see Helaman 10:4–5), showing forth unending patience and hoping in all things through the Atonement of our Savior Jesus Christ (see Moroni 8:26).

- **A concerted effort on their part is key.** Throughout the process, we must remember that it is imperative that the wayward accept responsibility and make some form of commitment to change. Real growth requires commitment. A regularly scheduled meeting to teach and nurture might be appropriate. We can follow through and be supportive in trying times, but we cannot force a commitment where there is no will to change.

As we work with those sheep who have wandered, let us all remember these consoling thoughts from the Prophet Joseph:

> The Prophet Joseph Smith declared—and he
> never taught a more comforting doctrine—that
> the eternal sealings of faithful parents and the

divine promises made to them for valiant service in the Cause of Truth, would save not only themselves, but likewise their posterity. Though some of the sheep may wander, the eye of the Shepherd is upon them, and sooner or later they will feel the tentacles of Divine Providence reaching out after them and drawing them back to the fold. Either in this life or the life to come, they will return. They will have to pay their debt to justice; they will suffer for their sins; and may tread a thorny path; but if it leads them at last, like the penitent Prodigal, to a loving and forgiving father's heart and home, the painful experience will not have been in vain. Pray for your careless and disobedient children; hold on to them with your faith. Hope on, trust on, till you see the salvation of God. (Orson F. Whitney, Conference Report, Apr. 1929, 110)

Brigham Young assured us:

Let the father and mother, who are members of this Church and Kingdom, take a righteous course, and strive with all their might never to do a wrong, but to do good all their lives; if they have one child or one hundred children, if they conduct themselves towards them as they should, binding them to the Lord by their faith and prayers, I care not where those children go, they are bound up to their parents by an everlasting tie, and no power of earth or hell can separate them from their parents in eternity; they will return again to the fountain from whence they sprang. (Quoted in Joseph Fielding Smith, *Doctrines of Salvation*, comp. Bruce R. McConkie, 3 vols. [Salt Lake City: Bookcraft, 1955], 2:90)

Elder Boyd K. Packer reminds us:

> The measure of our success as parents . . . will not rest solely on how our children turn out. That judgment would be just only if we could raise our families in a perfectly moral environment, and that now is not possible. . . .
> It is my conviction that those wicked influences one day will be overruled. . . .
> We cannot overemphasize the value of temple marriage, the binding ties of the sealing ordinance, and the standards of worthiness required of them. When parents keep the covenants they have made at the altar of the temple, their children will be forever bound to them." ("Our Moral Environment," *Ensign*, May 1992, 68)

Souls are precious. There can be no limit to our effort and desire to help everyone return to the presence of our Heavenly Father. This is our Savior's goal: to redeem all of God's children. The Prophet Joseph F. Smith taught:

> Jesus had not finished his work when his body was slain, neither did he finish it after his resurrection from the dead; although he had accomplished the purpose for which he then came to the earth, he had not fulfilled all his work. And when will he? Not until he has redeemed and saved every son and daughter of our father Adam that have been or ever will be born upon this earth to the end of time, except the sons of perdition. That is his mission. We will not finish our work until we have saved ourselves, and then not until we shall have saved all depending upon us; for we are to become saviors upon Mount Zion, as well as Christ. We are called to this mission. (*Gospel Doctrine: Selections*

from the Sermons and Writings of Joseph F. Smith, comp. John A. Widtsoe [Salt Lake City: Deseret Book, 1919], 442)

We are the under-shepherds to find and bless those who have lost their way. As we reach out to them in love, the Savior will comfort our aching hearts and eventually help us find "joy in the soul that repenteth" (D&C 18:13).

CHAPTER NINETEEN
COPING WITH GRIEF

*Come unto me, all ye that labour and are
heavy laden, and I will give you rest. Take my yoke
upon you, and learn of me; for I am meek and lowly in
heart: and ye shall find rest unto your souls. For
my yoke is easy, and my burden is light.*
—Matthew 11:28–30

The greatest of all sorrows comes with the passing of a loved one—for that event is marked with the signature of finality. There is no reversing of the tide. There is no turning back the clock—only looking forward with hope toward a future reunion in the world to come. Our Lord has provided for us in such moments of grief the transcendent blessings of comfort and peace bestowed through the Comforter, who is the Holy Ghost: "But the Comforter, which is the Holy Ghost, whom the Father will send in my name, he shall teach you all things, and bring all things to your remembrance, whatsoever I have said unto you. Peace I leave with you, my peace I give unto you: not as the world giveth, give I unto you. Let not your heart be troubled, neither let it be afraid" (John 14:26–27).

Prophetic Counsel. Declared Elder Russell M. Nelson:

> Comfort and peace! What divine and priceless gifts!
> Remarkably reassuring for those who encounter grief is the promised visitation of

the Holy Ghost—the divine Comforter—who
will provide hope and perfect love. And when
nourished by prayer, that hope and love will
endure until the end, when all saints shall dwell
with God. (See Moroni 8:26.)

These gifts extend to all who truly believe
in him, and are granted because of his infinite
love for us. His peace comes as we comprehend
his grace and act according to his will. It comes
from faith founded upon his infinite atonement.
To find that hope, that reassurance, and the
ability to carry on, the bereaved person will
seek to know the Lord and to serve him. It is
his atonement that will make our future bright,
regardless of the dark days inevitably encountered
on life's journey. (*The Gateway We Call Death*
[Salt Lake City: Deseret Book, 1995], x–xi)

A New Life. When a loved one passes away, a life recedes
into the shadows. But the memories linger on, and the influence
of that loved one retains its vitality as a blessing for the
grieving survivors who continue to pursue their destiny along
the pathway of mortality. In a true sense, there is no passing
away, for life goes on—sometimes in miraculous ways, as the
following true story from a priesthood brother illustrates:

I can recall the spring day long ago when my
mother departed with my father for the local
hospital. The hour had come for the arrival of the
long-awaited addition to our family. Excitement
was high. During that long evening of waiting,
my sister having also gone to the hospital with our
parents, I was entertained at the home of next-door
relatives where an older cousin played songs for me
on his guitar. A young lad at the time, I walked
home alone later that evening and retired to bed,

eager to learn by next morning of the forthcoming news.

During the night I recall being awakened from a deep sleep. Shifting silhouette figures appeared in the doorway of my bedroom, illuminated from behind by the light in the hallway. A voice called out. It was the voice of my father. The news was shocking, devastating. My mother had passed away in bringing a new life into the world.

Words are inadequate to express the depth of sorrow that settled over our family in the wake of such a loss. There was a pall of mourning over the whole community. The warmth of spring had been snuffed out. The seasons had shifted, and winter had returned. It was as if life were gasping for breath and for a renewal.

And yet there was a renewal—a miracle in the midst of heartbreak. A new life had come into our world. A choice new baby boy had entered the family circle. My mother had fulfilled her mission once again. Looking back at this reality after a lifetime of contemplation and pondering, I can see that my mother's mission still continued in her family. Her influence never left us.

What can you do to feel better at times of grief and bereavement? Here are few ideas to consider:

- **Seek to understand.** Dealing with death comes to every living soul save the very young. Grief comes with the mortal experience, because opposition in all things is part of the plan of happiness (see 2 Nephi 2:11). Grief provides an opportunity to grow with the process of overcoming and enduring well the challenges of life (see Ecclesiastes 1:18).
- **Reach out for help.** A time of grief is not a time to remain in isolation. Turn to loved ones who can show

empathy and understanding and can strengthen you and give you hope. In seeking the support of loved ones, remember that there is a balance to seek—a balance of comfort from family and friends on the one hand and closeness to the Lord on the other (see Proverbs 3:5–6). Priesthood power can assist with blessings that can heal us both temporally and spiritually (see D&C 107:18). The Savior can lighten the burden through the power of the Atonement. All our burdens can be laid at the feet of our Savior, who will make them seem light and bearable (see Matthew 11:28–30; Mosiah 24:14–15; Alma 33:23).

• **Choose a positive perspective.** Faith dispels grief in time. Remember that sooner or later things will be better as you rely on the Lord and do all that lies within your power to endure to the end (see D&C 123:17). You can be positive. Hope in our Savior will give you strength to carry on by faith and through trust (see Moroni 7:41; Alma 36:3). Remember that in every case of grief, the situation is far lighter than what the Savior went through in grieving over mankind during His atoning sacrifice (see D&C 122:8; 19:15–19).

• **Take active steps to dispel or dilute grief.** The arsenal of tools for dispelling or diluting grief is wonderful:

 • **Pray**—Prayer is part of living the gospel in every situation. Prayer is the power to bring down the blessings of heaven (see Psalm 102).

 • **Face it head on**—You can be of strong courage, not denying your loss but seeking to overcome it through faith and accepting comfort from loved ones and friends. Tears are natural; recognize your feelings and how to address them: "Be of good courage, and he shall strengthen your heart, all ye that hope in the Lord" (Psalm 31:24).

 • **Seek to serve**—When you turn yourself outward, looking to bless and serve, you receive the comfort of the Holy Spirit, and the pains within are often lightened or relieved (see Moroni 8:26).

• **Be tolerant**—Be tolerant of yourself and others as they deal with grief. Everyone is different. Everyone will not proceed at the same recovery rate, nor will their perception be the same. Simply be supporting, loving, and nonjudgmental. You can never know the depths of another's feelings. Don't compare yourself with others who have gone through a similar experience. Your life is yours to live; your triumphs over grief are your triumphs of strength and resolve.

Grief is an inescapable element of life, for death touches the circle of every individual sooner or later. But fellowship and service, comfort and reassurance, charity and support in the kingdom of God—all of these help to make grief less of a burden and more of a stepping stone to higher wisdom and thankfulness for the blessings of our Father in Heaven.

Grief and all of its companions (misery, woe, despair, sorrow, and the like) are part of the growing and testing time here upon the earth, and all of us will experience them. The questions are: How will we deal with it? How can we grow from it? How can we help others using the lessons we have learned? All things we experience on the earth are part of our learning opportunity to help us become perfect as Heavenly Father and His Son are perfect. Just as Job, Joseph Smith, and many of God's choice servants suffered, so must we all suffer in our own way, remembering always that Christ suffered and grieved for all mankind more than we can comprehend. Let us go forward and not backward, knowing the goodness of God and maintaining our hope through Christ as we look forward to a better time and place in the mansions of God that await us.

CHAPTER TWENTY
COPING WITH ABUSE

Behold, ye are little children and ye cannot
bear all things now; ye must grow in grace and in the
knowledge of the truth. Fear not, little children, for you are
mine, and I have overcome the world, and you are of them that
my Father hath given me; And none of them that
my Father hath given me shall be lost.
—D&C 50:40–42

Coping with being a victim of abuse is one of the most difficult things to be faced with. Our beloved Savior truly understands this, for He suffered all things in order to succor us when we are in the depths of our deepest sorrows and misery (see Alma 7:11–12). The oft uttered words "Why me?" and "This isn't fair!" ring out in pain from the victims as they express their anguish. But even innocent victims of others' misdeeds can find a way to happiness and joy.

The following story, shared by a former mission president, demonstrates the principles of how we can overcome the devastating effects of abuse and find renewed peace, hope, and happiness:

> It all began in the mission field when a young sister missionary was struggling. The sister was new and was having difficulty coping with the rigors of missionary work. Her companion was frustrated and didn't know what to do. She was unable to get to the root of the problem. My

initial interview with the sister was normal in that she was a little fearful and yet seemed okay. I had the assistants and training sisters make special visits to the companionship. But still this sister was unable to meet people and open her mouth. Finally one day she simply ran from her companion and returned to the apartment. The assistants called and suggested I meet with her immediately. Zone interviews were that week. She came in and sat down, and when I began to ask how things were going, she burst into tears. I too didn't know what to do. The good thing is the Spirit did. As she wept I mentioned it was okay to cry and suggested she sit for a while as I stepped outside for a moment. As I stood, I raised my hand to smooth out my hair, and at that moment she looked up and immediately cowered as I had raised my hand to my head. Then I knew. I sat down and said how sorry I was for her.

As we began to visit, I asked her if her abuse was physical and she whispered yes. Then I asked if it was also sexual, and she whispered yes. My heart was aching. I pleaded for the Lord to bless her and help her. I then asked if it was her father and again she whispered yes. We visited at length. I gave her a priesthood blessing. She responded well and seemed to feel better. I asked if she wanted to be happy. With a ray of hope she responded with, "I'll do anything to be happy again." After a long discussion about abuse and sin and reassuring her that this was not her fault, I suggested that we move forward on the road to happiness.

We visited often. Over time her countenance changed. Through the grace of God and the atoning sacrifice of our Savior, she was nurtured of the Lord and was healed (see Alma 7:11–12). She became a wonderful missionary. She was effervescent and enthusiastic in the work. Everyone loved being her companion. It was a miracle. She returned home after her mission and was married and had a wonderful family.

One of the most difficult aspects of being a victim is that the victim must sometimes make the effort to address the sin and be the initiator in the repentance and forgiveness process. This is difficult and seems unfair, yet sometimes it is absolutely necessary. When we don't make the effort to forgive and seek help from others, it will be difficult to ever feel good again. But those who do make the effort with courage and faith will realize the dream in due time—renewed peace and hope and happiness.

Here are some things to consider when dealing with abuse: Turn to the Lord, fasting and praying for direction and comfort and searching and feasting upon the word of the Lord. Seek counsel and support from priesthood leaders, qualified professionals, and friends and family. Follow the counsel of the living prophets. Study and apply the principles in the conference talk by Elder Richard G. Scott, "To Heal the Shattering Consequences of Abuse" (*Ensign,* May 2008, 40–43), which confirms that the power of healing is inherent in the Atonement of Jesus Christ.

How can one ever recover that feeling of wholeness and goodness after abuse? The answer is through living the gospel of Jesus Christ with complete devotion, through kneeling in humble prayer at the feet of the Almighty to ask for peace, through experiencing the healing balm of the Atonement, and through receiving the hope and vision of a better world of glory and of celestial rest that lies ahead. "Bring them hither and I will heal them," said the Lord, "for I have compassion upon you; my bowels are filled with mercy" (3 Nephi 17:7).

CHAPTER TWENTY-ONE
FOCUSING ON CHERISHED RELATIONSHIPS

*And for their sakes I sanctify
myself, that they also might be sanctified
through the truth.
—John 17:19*

Relationships are one of the most rewarding yet challenging aspects of life. Our greatest joys derive from relationships with loved ones that are rewarding and satisfying, and yet nothing is quite so disconcerting as an important relationship with major problems. That kind of situation creates a state of heartache and pain that just never seems to go away—and we end up feeling miserable until things can be resolved.

Earth life and all of its joys are built upon relationships. The association and involvement with others—spouse, family, friends, and associates—constitutes one of life's supreme values. Marriage, family, school, and the workplace become enjoyable when there are positive, meaningful relationships there. Life's enduring memories are usually associated with the people we care about. These relationships make life full and wonderful when they are harmonious and vibrant—or empty and miserable when they are hurtful and incomplete. The moments and memories we have with a parent, spouse, family member, loving friend, or other close associate can provide relief from our difficulties and make life sweetly fulfilling.

Our actions and attitudes determine the fulfillment and success we enjoy in relationships. Positive attitudes and actions nurture relationships. Healthy relationships are constructive, pure, and harmonious. When we learn to give of ourselves, our time, and our resources, we find that our relationships reap the benefits of our efforts. Successful relationships become a source of joy and happiness in life.

The first and most important relationship is with our Heavenly Father and our Savior Jesus Christ. We come to know, love, trust, respect, and reverence our God and His Only Begotten Son: "And this is life eternal, that they might know thee the only true God, and Jesus Christ, whom thou hast sent" (John 17:3). This will be the foundation of all other relationships.

Our association and connection with our brothers and sisters—like our relationship with Heavenly Father and Jesus—is based upon love. True love is expressed as we show concern for others and their well-being. We then build relationships based upon trust, respect and devotion. Our highest goal should be to love our fellowmen, for this manifests our love for God (see John 13:34–35; 1 John 4:20).

Prophetic Counsel. Elder Jeffrey R. Holland reminded us, "We should try to be more constant and unfailing, more longsuffering and kind, less envious and puffed up in our relationships with others. As Christ lived so should we live, and as Christ loved so should we love" (*Christ and the New Covenant: The Messianic Message of the Book of Mormon* [Salt Lake City: Deseret Book, 1997], 336–37). President Ezra Taft Benson said, "To be like Christ should be the righteous aspiration of every member of the Church. We should act as He would act in our relationships with others" (*Come unto Christ* [Salt Lake City: Deseret Book, 1983], 52). Elder Joseph B. Wirthlin encouraged us with these words:

> I believe that the little things are of great importance in our relationship with ourselves, in our relationships with others, and in our relationship with God. . . .

Do we take the time to remember the simple courtesies that are so important in building relationships with others? Do we remember the smile, the compliment, the positive note, and the word of encouragement? We should do these things without hesitation. They should be a part of our everyday manner. (*Finding Peace in Our Lives* [Salt Lake City: Deseret Book, 1995], 59–60)

Of all the relationships in the world, the relationship between man and woman is the most rewarding and the most challenging. In marriage, as in all relationships, there are principles that foster good feelings and preserve enduring harmony. Consider the following illustration:

Tom and Sally were struggling. Sally called a friend who was a marriage counselor and said, "We've got problems." Tom was willing to work on things, but their relationship had suffered so many setbacks that communication was difficult. They wanted to stay together; after all, they had three beautiful children, but things were so stressed—financial problems, disagreements over discipline, the way each responded to the other with fault-finding and negative comments. Yes, their relationship was in trouble.

No one else seemed to notice. They put on a good front. They were good parents, but the real concern was whether they were working on being a good husband and a good wife. They needed help—so they tried. That is the key. They tried to have a better relationship, so the appointment with the counselor was made.

As the counselor visited with Tom and Sally, they vented all their problems. Fault-finding was apparent. That's when the counselor said, "Do you really want to be happy? Are you willing to change? Are you willing to try to build back your relationship like it was when you were first married?" Through tears, they both agreed. Humility precedes a change of heart as well as action. The counselor continued. They discussed some things to help improve their relationship:

- Spend time together doing fun things.
- Talk and listen to each other with real intent.
- Agree on family values. There can never be unity or a good strong relationship without common values.
- Be each other's best friend. Talk about life and fun things you have done and those special moments that bring memories of joy.
- Go on a trip together, just the two of you. Husbands and wives need to nurture each other—not just the children.
- Make a plan *together* for your life *together*, and then make it happen.

Following the visit, they realized that the problems in their relationship had begun slowly, almost insidiously. As they reminisced about their dating and all the fun times they had had, it seemed as if a veil, even a mist of darkness, lifted. They looked at the good, not the bad. Commitments were made. Smiles returned to their faces. They cultivated the Spirit by praying more faithfully and bringing their family together more regularly for scripture reading and spiritual nourishment. Sure it took time, but it happened. They paid the price. Their relationship flourished. They spent the time to help each other be happy, and they were happy. There was no selfishness, the destroyer of all relationships. Instead, there was concern for each other.

The surprising thing is that their relationship with their children and their friends improved as well. Honesty, humility, commitment, and devoted service—all of these helped Tom and Sally build and maintain relationships of vitality and joy.

Here are some ideas for you to consider as you strive to improve your relationships with others in keeping with the Golden Rule: "Therefore all things whatsoever ye would that men should do to you, do ye even so to them . . ." (Matthew 7:12):

- **Relationships are like gardens: They require constant nurture.** You can cultivate the soil of common ground and mutual interests in your relationships, constantly clearing back the weeds of misunderstanding and jealousy and always supplying the nutrients of encouragement, hope, and positive support. In the spirit of charity, you can then add the moisture of love, cleansing forgiveness, and compassion, plus the sunshine of enthusiasm and energy. From all this, you can harvest the fruit of harmony, balance, peace, and joy, and leave behind the good seeds of honesty and integrity for the coming generations. What is the model for such a plan of nurture? It is the loving kindness of our Father in Heaven and His Son, Jesus Christ.
- **Relationships are based on many small acts of initiative.** The demonstration of trust and love, the example of dependability and respect, the kindness of charity and benevolence, the loyalty of keeping promises and withholding all gossip, and the support of encouragement and praise—these are the keys to enduring relationships. Said Thomas Aquinas: "The happy man needs friends . . . not, indeed, to make use of them, since he suffices himself, nor to delight in them, since he possesses perfect delight in the operation of virtue, but for the purpose of a good operation, namely, that he may do good to them, that he

may delight in seeing them do good, and again that he may be helped by them in his good work."

• **Some relationships are sacred.** Relationships with parents, spouse, children, and God are of paramount importance in life. Where the relationship between husband and wife is grounded in commitment, shared vision, forgiving tenderness, and abiding love, all things are possible on the pathway to success and harmony. We must all honor our parents—no matter what the circumstances—for that is the word from Sinai (see Exodus 20:12), and no duty or commission in life is higher than the parents' sacred obligation to work for the blessing and good of their children in every way. Where the relationship with Heavenly Father and our Savior Jesus Christ is based on humility, gratitude, honor, and obedience, there will be peace and quiet joy in rich abundance. In all of these things, you can work to cultivate and maintain tender relationships and find the blessings of the Spirit lifting and strengthening your life and the lives of your loved ones.

Daily entries in each family's book of life could be about things that have happened to strengthen their relationships. The key is to care for others and work together to make the relationship strong so that it can endure the trials and tribulations of life. Through faith and devoted effort we can attain all worthy goals—including close and endearing relationships. Truly our enduring relationships of trust and love bring joy to life—even in the midst of adversity.

CHAPTER TWENTY-TWO
FOCUSING ON PREPARING CHILDREN TO FACE THE FUTURE

*I have no greater joy than to hear that
my children walk in truth.*
—3 John 1:4

Of all the tasks on earth, nothing is so difficult or so rewarding as raising a child. The trials seem almost overwhelming and the joys simply exhilarating. Our joy surely is in our posterity. The question is, what can we do to help them grow without so many crises? What can we do to help prevent problems that need not occur? What can we do to help them become truly converted to the gospel of Jesus Christ and have a desire to live it throughout their lives? What can we do to help them be prepared to share the gospel and keep the sacred covenants of the temple? What can we do to help prepare them for marriage and their future families? Raising children is the most important thing we, as parents, will ever do. These are our eternal roles that will go on through all eternity as we become worthy of exaltation.

Parents have the responsibility of providing their children with food, clothing, and shelter. They also have the responsibility to help keep their children on the straight and narrow path, teaching them to avoid contention, for contention is of the devil (see 3 Nephi 11:29). The major role of parents is to teach their children the principles of righteousness (see Moses 6:57–58). "Train up a child in the way he should go: and when he is old, he will not depart from it" (Proverbs 22:6). This proverb extends a promise—a grand promise of lasting value. We can therefore make a plan to teach by precept and example the gospel of Jesus Christ to our children in their early years.

How is this done? Within your family you can establish righteous traditions: family prayer, family scripture study, family home evening, family council, family blessings and interviews, and family vacations that build family unity. You can make your home a place of safety—a place of refuge from the storms of life. It is critical never to hurt, belittle, or in any way abuse a child, for children are pure and seek love and learning from their parents and other adults. For those who fail in this stewardship, or lapse into abuse, the consequences are severe. On the other hand, the joy of success in parenting is boundless.

This responsibility of raising a family is serious business. It has eternal consequences. Nothing has greater priority in life than raising children to be righteous, self-reliant adults capable of using their agency wisely—a daunting task filled with boundless emotions of concern and yet overflowing with the inexpressible joys of seeing a child grow and become all that he or she can be.

Prophetic Counsel. In explaining the responsibilities parents have to their children, President Ezra Taft Benson had this counsel for mothers that can apply to fathers, as well:

> Teach children gospel principles. Teach them it pays to be good. Teach them there is no safety in sin. Teach them a love for the gospel of Jesus Christ and a testimony of its divinity.
>
> Teach your sons and daughters modesty, and teach them to respect manhood and womanhood. Teach your children sexual purity, proper dating standards, temple marriage, missionary service, and the importance of accepting and magnifying Church callings.
>
> Teach them a love for work and the value of a good education.
>
> Teach them the importance of the right kind of entertainment, including appropriate movies

and videos and music and books and magazines. Discuss the evils of pornography and drugs, and teach them the value of living the clean life.

Yes, mothers, teach your children the gospel in your own home, at your own fireside. This is the most effective teaching that your children will ever receive. This is the Lord's way of teaching. The Church cannot teach like you can. The school cannot. The day-care center cannot. But you can, and the Lord will sustain you. Your children will remember your teachings forever, and when they are old, they will not depart from them. (See Prov. 22:6) . . .

This kind of heavenly, motherly teaching takes time—lots of time. It cannot be done effectively part-time. It must be done all the time in order to save and exalt your children. This is your divine calling.

Your teenage children also need that same kind of love and attention. It seems easier for many mothers and fathers to express and show their love to their children when they are young, but more difficult when they are older. Work at this prayerfully. There need be no generation gap. And the key is love. Our young people need love and attention, not indulgence. They need empathy and understanding, not indifference from mothers and fathers. They need the parents' time. A mother's kindly teachings and her love for and confidence in a teenage son or daughter can literally save them from a wicked world. (*Come, Listen to a Prophet's Voice* [Salt Lake City: Deseret Book, 1990], 35–36)

Here are some ideas you can consider in raising your children in the midst of the hectic world in which we live:

- **Make your children the center of your life.** They are your highest priority. They are more important than fame, professional acclaim, or fortune. "No other success can compensate for failure in the home" (quoting J.E. McCulloh, *Home: The Savior of Civilization* [1924], 42: in CR, Apr. 1935, 116) is the famous maxim taught by President David O. McKay. Children deserve your time, in terms of both quality and quantity. Spending caring time with them abundantly will generate lasting memories and prove you truly care. They need to know that you are their refuge and their support, their mentor and their friend, their source of encouragement and comfort—no matter what.

- **Make the home the most important venue for your children.** The home should be a refuge for children, a place of peace and security, the center of their lives. The home should be the gathering place for daily scripture sessions, pleasant mealtimes, weekly family home evenings, and other special family activities. The home should be a place where children can feel at ease in welcoming their friends—a place more appealing than any other place on earth.

- **Make love the center of the home.** Here are ten of the many faces of love and suggestions for applying them to your relationship with your children:

  - **Love is constant**—Show love often. Always show acceptance for your children.

  - **Love listens**—Nothing will induce feelings of self-confidence and self-regard in a child more than a sense of being listened to.

  - **Love is flexible**—Each child is different; loving them takes a customized approach for each.

  - **Love looks for the good**—Put emphasis on catching your children doing things right. Praise sincerely and frequently, always being specific about what is admirable.

  - **Love is specific**—Take time to help your children understand specifically what is expected of them regarding their attitudes and behaviors.

- **Love is balanced**—Balance your children's need for strong discipline with their need to learn to make responsible choices. Henry Ward Beecher noted, "You cannot teach a child to take care of himself unless you let him try to take care of himself. He will make mistakes; and out of these mistakes will come his wisdom."
- **Love accepts the individual**—Always separate behavior from the individual. You accept your children but not always everything they do. Avoid labeling them; instead, identify the behaviors that need to improve.
- **Love takes the long view**—Never chastise your children without offering them enough of the "balm of love" to ensure your relationship will still be good. There are dozens of ways to say "no" without causing ill feelings or lasting grudges.
- **Love measures carefully**—Give your children specific jobs to do and expect good performance. Help them evaluate their progress. Have suitable rewards for reaching goals.
- **Love is patient**—Never forget that your children are young and need time to become mature and responsible.
- **Teach your children eternal principles.** Teach them correct principles based on the scriptures and the words of the living prophets of the Lord. Help them build a foundation based on eternal principles. Help them establish a gospel value system to govern their behavior. Remember that agreed-upon values bring unity to the family. Worship together. Attend church meetings together. Find regular ways for the family to show devotion and reverence for God and life. Said Eleanor Roosevelt: "If you can give your children a trust in God, they will have one sure way of meeting all the uncertainties of existence."

As parents and loving mentors, we can all seek to be tender, patient, and understanding. The opportunity to make a difference in one child's life can be fleeting—unless we make full and timely use of it.

Libraries are full of books on how to raise children. In this short treatment of a key subject, we have attempted to offer a few suggestions to help all of us do better in raising our children. Let us do all that we can to see that all children have the opportunity to grow up with love and high standards. The eternal rewards are measureless. As the Apostle John stated: "I have no greater joy than to hear that my children walk in truth" (3 John 1:4). With that joy, we can all feel good, even when things seem bad.

PART THREE:
SAFE HARBOR

With God all things are possible.
—Matthew 19:26

Who are we? Each man, woman, and child is created after the image of the Father, with a divine destiny of becoming like Him through the power of the Atonement and the blessings of the plan of happiness. The purpose of our mortal life is to receive a physical tabernacle and show ourselves worthy of returning home once again, to live with our families forever in joy and glory. The trials and tribulations of life cannot eclipse the truth of who we really are. Knowing this, we can always look on the bright side—being filled with light in a world that sometimes abounds in shadows and darkness. The Savior said, "If thy whole body therefore be full of light, having no part dark, the whole shall be full of light, as when the bright shining of a candle doth give thee light" (Luke 11:36). In this final section, let us examine some ways to enhance the light of our everyday lives.

CHAPTER TWENTY-THREE
ACHIEVING BALANCE IN LIFE

*And it came to pass that we lived after
the manner of happiness.*
—*2 Nephi 5:27*

Balance is about renewal, rejuvenation. It's about tending to our own needs so we are better prepared to serve others. Refreshing our lives is critical to our well-being—the physical, mental, social, intellectual, and spiritual need to be in balance. Too much of one thing will soon tire our heart, deflating the enjoyment previously received. Too much fun makes no fun at all. Too much work makes work drudgery. The Lord does not require us to do more than is expected—but we need to organize every needful thing so that everything is in balance, leaving time for renewal as well as work.

Prophetic Counsel. President Harold B. Lee said: "Because the Latter-day Saints realize that the spiritual, mental and physical factors of life must be balanced in order to have a fulness of life, they have been prepared to meet the emergencies of life and do not falter under the strain, no matter how great it may be" (*Decisions for Successful Living* [Salt Lake City: Deseret Book, 1973], 70). President Gordon B. Hinckley counseled: "Keep balance in your lives. Beware of obsession. Beware of narrowness. Let your interests range over many good fields while working with growing strength in the field of your own profession" (*Teachings of Gordon B. Hinckley* [Salt Lake City: Deseret Book, 1997], 32–33).

In order to achieve the kind of balance that will enable you to effectively deal with the complexities of life, you might consider the following ideas and actions:

- **Set your priorities in order.** There is wisdom in understanding the difference between gratification on the one hand and joy (or wholesome pleasure) on the other. Gratification is fleeting and ephemeral; joy is enduring. Gratification is of the surface; joy is of the soul. Gratification is self-oriented; joy is others-oriented and depends on enduring and warm relationships. Gratification relates to appetite; joy relates to service. Gratification is titillating; joy is nourishing. You can readily tell the difference between gratification and joy: when it ends leaving only hunger and often remorse, then it was an instance of gratification; when it ends and there remains a happy memory and hope for its return, then it was an instance of joy (wholesome pleasure).
- **Understanding this difference will help you find perspective:** You feed your body in order to live, but you feed your soul in order to live well. You can attend to the needs of the moment, but at the same time you set your long-range goals based on lasting values of harmony, peace, and joy. Following this principle, you can therefore aspire to a good balance: enjoying the simple pleasures of life—a hearty meal together with family or friends, a beautiful sunset, a moment of peace, endearing time together with your spouse, even caring tenderly for a pet—while looking beyond the moment to the eternal blessings for the faithful and valiant.
- **We can all strive to align ourselves with gospel principles.** We can anchor ourselves in the Lord Jesus Christ and the rock of His enduring principles, thereby securing for ourselves a life of joy—no matter what happens.
- **Go through an honest reality check of your condition.** What are the symptoms of a pleasure-seeking personality? Savoring the quest for endless variety and thriving on the

ceaseless flux of shifting fads, fancies, and flavors. The selfish pleasure-seeker is too often blind to the vital needs of family, too often deaf to the whispers of loved ones who want only lasting relationships and enduring harmony and love. On the other hand, a joy-seeking personality is characterized by savoring enduring relationships, harmony, balance, peace, and the quest to honor and abide by enduring principles and values. Which personality best describes you? Where do you spend your time? In activities that gratify or in activities that build relationships and contribute to harmony, balance, and peace? You can choose the latter and find immense joy in living according to eternal principles.

• **Achieve authentic balance.** By planning your agenda with care, you can focus on wholesome, uplifting activities as a source of genuine pleasure. Adjust your perspective, keeping your view of life clear so that you can find pleasure in your service in the Church, in the home, and in the workplace—as well as in your wholesome hobbies and avocations. In balancing your life, you can plan for enjoyable, worthwhile activities that add excitement by contributing to a higher quality of life for yourself and those around you. Use your time and talents to bring about much good for the most people possible.

It is important to seek balance in our lives. Life can be hard—at least when we perceive it to be so—and to achieve balance we must put all things in their proper place. We should experience pleasure in life, and we should make it a positive and uplifting experience—not just an indulgent moment to tantalize our senses. A truly balanced life is the result of following gospel principles and cultivating a Christlike character and manner of living, enriched through a balanced harmony of wholesome and pleasurable activities. Life can be good if we make it so by relying on the Lord and finding balance—even when things seem bad.

CHAPTER TWENTY-FOUR
ENHANCING SELF-ESTEEM

And behold, ye are the children of the
prophets; . . . ye are the children of the covenant.
—3 Nephi 20:25–26

How we look at ourselves is the inner key to enhancing our feelings of self-esteem, self-worth, and self-respect. Having a positive image of ourselves has a profound influence on our manner of living. When we esteem ourselves as children of God, we are filled with hope about what we can accomplish and become. We understand who we really are—the literal children of God the Eternal Father, with a divine heritage and capability of becoming like Him. We have worth. We were born to be great.

We should help everyone by precept and example—including ourselves, and especially our children—to increase self-esteem (believing in oneself), self-worth (placing value in self), and self-respect (having regard for self). All of these should be enhanced by the recognition that we have worth in and through the Lord—not just because of what we might do or accomplish, but because we have an inborn divine potential that can, through humility, faith, and good works, transform us into beings like unto our Father and His Only Begotten Son, Jesus Christ (see Acts 17:28–29; Romans 8:16; 3 Nephi 12:48; 27:27).

Prophetic Counsel. Elder James E. Faust said this about self-esteem in our personal growth: "Self-esteem goes to the very heart of our personal growth and accomplishment. Self-esteem is the glue that holds together our self-reliance, our self-control, our self-approval or disapproval, and keeps all self-defense mechanisms secure. It is a protection against excessive self-deception, self-distrust, self-reproach, and plain, old-fashioned selfishness" (*Reach Up for the Light* [Salt Lake City: Deseret Book, 1990], 31).

If you are seeking to enhance your self-esteem and help your loved ones follow your example, consider the following ideas:

- **Remember who you really are.** Think of yourself, no matter what your circumstances, as a child of God. Knowing your divine parentage will give you increased courage and self-respect. Albert Schweitzer taught: "Every man has to seek in his own way to make his own self more noble and to realize his own true worth." To help in this process, pray for understanding and strength. Heavenly Father knows you best. Seek strength from Him.
- **Align yourself with principles of respect and honor.** The key is to cultivate enduring traits such as honesty, integrity, humility, creativity, and love of others. You are strengthened by the noble values you espouse. On the other hand, those who align themselves with empty fads, shallow pleasures, and passing fancies will come to think of themselves as mere phantoms of humanity, with no continuity or lasting value. Thus, the importance of recognizing your own potential for becoming even as Christ is (see 3 Nephi 27:27). Strive to be upright and valiant. Take a moment to ponder the things you have done in life that are noble and that demonstrate accomplishment—not just a few but a hundred! The results of this exercise will amaze you—every individual has accomplished much of worth in life.
- **Think lofty thoughts.** The poet Goethe counseled: "For a man to achieve all that is demanded of him, he must

regard himself as greater than he is." Fill your mind with uplifting ideas, thoughts, and dreams. You think of yourself as a person of respect—because you *are* a person of respect, someone who cultivates spiritual aspirations and positive thoughts and actions, as opposed to someone who thinks low thoughts and demeaning ideas. What you think is a measure of your esteem.

- **Establish a pattern of actions that generate self-esteem, self-worth, and self-respect.** Here are some possibilities (you may be able to add many others):
  - **Seek to grow continuously**—The following regimen feels good and leads to amazing results: stay on the learning track (reading the scriptures and other good books, attending classes, expanding your mind and understanding), optimize your health (exercising regularly, eating prudently, cultivating a healthy lifestyle), upgrade your appearance (dressing in a way that will enhance your appearance—not necessarily extravagantly, but attractively), stay active (avoiding passive obsessions, such as endless television consumption or ceaseless ingesting of questionable reading materials or vapid music, and instead using wisdom in choosing enriching and inspirational pastimes that add to your internal wealth and vitality), be kind to yourself (never putting yourself down with demeaning self-judgment), and, finally, be willing to change for the better. When you fall short of your potential and do something wrong, admit it and rise above it, asking forgiveness of anyone you might have offended. You will be stronger for it, and you will gain self-respect and respect from others.
  - **Cultivate lasting friendships**—There is wisdom in spending time with people who respect you and who will listen to you. Nothing increases self-worth more than discovering someone who is willing to listen—truly listen—and then respond with kindness and encouragement. In spending time with such a person,

you cultivate the language of respect (learning to express yourself with clarity and correctness, using positive language and enhancing your vocabulary on a regular basis, understanding that your speech is a measure of your self-esteem). Compliment and praise others sincerely and often, reaching out to people who lack a positive self-image and doing all in your power to lift their spirits, restore hope, and give them confidence to go on. In this process, your own sense of self-worth will improve and blossom. Then look around at the people who depend on you for guidance—your children, your neighbors, your team members at work—and spend time truly listening to their needs, desires, and challenges. You will boost their self-confidence immeasurably, and this will, in turn, boost yours as well. Focus on solutions rather than condemnation, be creative and resourceful rather than judgmental, and learn to spread positive images of others and avoid all gossip. Dispensing hope and encouragement to others will enhance their self-worth and self-confidence—as well as your own.

• **Be family centered**—One way to lay a solid foundation for lasting self-esteem is to study the lives of your forebears, identifying those honorable souls in your family line who have transcended obstacles and met challenges with triumph. View yourself as a descendant of noble stock with a responsibility to carry on a good tradition. Then follow through by making your family the center of your life. The legacy of honesty, peace, harmony, and joy you leave for the new generation will become the measure of your self-worth and self-respect. Nothing will give you more self-respect than success with this duty and opportunity.

It is vital that we understand the significance of building our own and others' self-esteem, self-worth, and self-respect.

Success in the family, school, and society can often be traced to these feelings. The ways we address, characterize, and relate to children will determine the way their self-respect unfolds. The Savior addressed His children with appellations and characterizations of nobility and grand potential:

> And behold, ye are the children of the prophets; and ye are of the house of Israel; and ye are of the covenant which the Father made with your fathers, saying unto Abraham: And in thy seed shall all the kindreds of the earth be blessed.
>
> The Father having raised me up unto you first, and sent me to bless you in turning away every one of you from his iniquities; and this because ye are the children of the covenant—
>
> And after that ye were blessed then fulfilleth the Father the covenant which he made with Abraham, saying: In thy seed shall all the kindreds of the earth be blessed. (3 Nephi 20:25–27)

Following this example, let us teach ourselves and our families who we really are—and who all individuals are who come into Christ's fold: "children of the prophets" and "children of the covenant"—God's chosen people to bless the world. Living up to that commission is the essence of genuine self-esteem, self-worth, and self-respect, and it will cause us to feel good about ourselves regardless of how bad things seem to be.

CHAPTER TWENTY-FIVE
INCREASING SELF-CONTROL

But this much I can tell you, that if
ye do not watch yourselves, and your thoughts, and
your words, and your deeds, and observe the commandments
of God, and continue in the faith . . . even unto the
end of your lives, ye must perish. And now, O
man, remember and perish not.
—Mosiah 4:30

Everyone, no matter how old, has to fight the ongoing struggle to cultivate and maintain self-control. Learning to control one's emotions and actions is most difficult. Yet, one of the main purposes to this earth life is to learn to make the body subject to the spirit and to follow the principles of the gospel rather than responding only to appetite and emotion. Self-control is a vital part of self-mastery and therefore of gaining self-confidence and achieving self-reliance. Many of society's difficulties arise because so many people have never learned discipline. Benjamin Franklin got it right: "Would you live with ease, do what you ought, and not what you please." In the spiritual realm, Elder James E. Faust made clear our responsibility as disciples of the Savior: "Self-discipline and self-control are consistent and permanent characteristics of the followers of Jesus" (*To Reach Even unto You* [Salt Lake City: Deseret Book, 1990], 114).

When we increase our self-control—exhibiting a positive attitude, a trust within, a certainty of our abilities, a hope and assurance that we can perform well—we indeed have self-confidence and the capacity for self-reliance. We can depend on ourselves to do what is expected of us. People who have this quality—even though they may not have achieved mastery in all aspects of their lives—have the ability to succeed in difficult situations. When we truly believe in ourselves, we will always do better. One of the great things we can do for others, especially our children, is to help them gain self-confidence. This will contribute, in turn, to their resourcefulness and self-reliance—especially as they learn to depend on the Lord and follow the promptings of His Spirit.

Listed below are several things you can do to help yourself and others gain a higher measure of self-control in life:

- **Build a strong foundation based on gospel principles for positive action.** As we have stressed throughout this book, you have the power to choose—you can choose to keep commitments and to gain self-control. Understanding the doctrines and principles of the gospel will empower you: the Atonement, your divine nature, the power of the Spirit, confidence that the Lord will provide a way, the love of God, and faith in Jesus Christ—all of these will bless your life and give you control over your forward motion toward eternal life.

- **Understand the promises and consequences.** There is no victory as sweet as the victory over self. Said Milton: "He who reigns within himself, and rules passions, desires and fears is more than a king."

- **Empower a team around you.** Tell others of your plans. Enlist their support. When you feel you need more strength, call for help—that's not a sign of weakness but of wisdom. Involve your family—make it a goal to learn self-control together. James M. Roche hit it on the head: "If a child does not learn discipline and responsibility in the home, he will not learn it elsewhere." You can even commit yourself to developing self-control for the benefit and well-being of your loved ones and others around you. That will motivate you to achieve your goal.

- **Make it a way of life.** Give it time. Think of it as a process. Perfect self-control takes time to develop. Practice with the small things—doing them well will build up your confidence. Train yourself and others to be obedient—thus increasing your self-control. A. J. Cronin counseled: "The virtue of all achievement is victory over oneself. Those who know this victory can never know defeat."

Prophetic Counsel. Without self-control we can never gain self-mastery, and we will not feel good about life or about ourselves. President David O. McKay taught: "Self-mastery [is] mastery over temper in the home; mastery over quick speech, hasty condemnation, controlling the tongue, and thus saving heartaches, injured feelings; mastery over the appetite, controlling an appetite which is God-given, but keeping it within bounds—there is no gourmandizing or injuring the body, weakening it; mastery over the passions, that too, a God-given gift. But how many millions prostitute it because they lack self-control?" (*Man May Know for Himself: Teachings of President David O. McKay*, comp. Clare Middlemiss [Salt Lake City: Deseret Book, 1967], 256–57).

Being a Good Sport. The following story shared by a father is a case study in learning self-control:

> I played ball all my life. I loved athletics. I enjoyed the thrill of competition. There was just one problem: the men in the striped shirts—the referees. They were the judge, the jury, and often the ones that decided the outcome of the game. We as spectators become the observers who yell and scream for our team—and at the man with the whistle. After my playing days, I became a true "fan"—you know, the one who protects the home team by yelling at those "refs."

As my children grew up, they too became athletes—state champions, all-state honors, all-American honors—and I was their personal protector, so I continued to scream at the referees. It often embarrassed the children. I would be good for a while, and then I would get upset and lose my self-control . . . not really bad, never shouting obscenities, mind you, just riding the referees, telling them to do better. Still, it showed a lack of dignity, manners, and true compassion and love for my fellow men. I was wrong. I needed to change. I needed to gain self-control.

I set a goal—I would exercise good sportsmanship and compassion for all—especially at ball games. My desire was strong. My plan was to pray before each game to be a "good sport" and be dignified at all times. My children and my wife couldn't believe it. I became a true gentleman. I had gained self-control. I was so pleased.

One day I attended a basketball game of our youngest daughter. I was doing just fine until the referee made a horrible mistake—at least in my eyes—and I yelled out, "Come on, ref, get in the game!" My older daughter said, "Dad, did you forget to pray?" I dropped my head, realizing that I *had* forgotten. I left the game, found a quiet place outside, and said a little prayer. I returned to the game, and sure enough, I behaved like a true gentleman again, dignified in every way. So here's what you have to do to gain self-control: set a goal, make a plan, get the support of family and friends, and ask for support from above. Then you can gain self-control. Trust me.

Self-control and discipline will not only bring success but also a sense of joy in knowing we are in control of our destiny. Let us make a commitment today, saying, "I have the power to discipline my life and gain self-control." Self-control is liberating. Seneca confirmed it when he taught: "No man is free who cannot command himself." Self-control takes time and effort, but with time it can be deepened and mastered. The keys are hope, faith, and leaning upon the Lord. "Jesus said unto him, If thou canst believe, all things are possible to him that believeth" (Mark 9:23). And again, "But Jesus beheld them, and said unto them, With men this is impossible; but with God all things are possible" (Matthew 19:26). Therefore, let us help ourselves—and everyone else—to develop self-control and the resulting self-reliance. Doing so will ensure that we will feel good, even when things seem bad.

CHAPTER TWENTY-SIX
DEFINING AND ATTAINING SUCCESS

O Lord, wilt thou comfort my soul,
and give unto me success, and also my fellow
laborers who are with me.
—Alma 31:32

All of us—individuals, families, groups, businesses, and governments—want to succeed. When we achieve important goals, we feel successful. Success seems to be the measurement in life. But what is success? What really matters? What are the genuine measurements of success? Success can be achieved in a variety of arenas, such as family, Church work, school, sports, business, media—and the list goes on. It is sad that the value system of the world looks at money, status, and fame as the criteria for success. We can remember to look at what truly matters most—true happiness, the well-being of our families, and eternal life—and then seek after these things. It would be well to evaluate our definitions of success for all the facets of our lives and then bring our goals and objectives into alignment with eternal principles and values.

Happiness is everyone's goal here upon the earth. Everyone wants to feel good and enjoy life, but many people do not know the one sure way to achieve happiness: keep the commandments. When we keep the commandments, we are blessed in all things that matter most, and we receive the ultimate reward of dwelling with God in never-ending happiness. This is true success. Let us therefore set our goals using plans to keep the commandments (see Mosiah 2:41). As we increase our faith, have an attitude of hope, and fill our lives with charity, we will abound in good works. Is not this success? We can assist in the work of the Lord with faith, hope, and charity (see D&C 12:8). Is not this success? In the work-a-day world, correct principles and Christlike attributes will always set us apart as people to be respected and admired. Let us seek to do these things.

Prophetic Counsel. President Howard W. Hunter taught:

> Ambition must be properly directed if we are to find true success. A man must have the ambition to succeed if he is to keep faith with himself, but ambition must be properly directed, not associated with evil, and the motivation must come from a worthy purpose. Joy and happiness in life are promised to those who have the right kind of success. We know that eternal joy is the purpose of man's creation, for the Lord said: "Men are, that they might have joy" (2 Nephi 2:25). (*The Teachings of Howard W. Hunter,* ed. Clyde J. Williams [Salt Lake City: Bookcraft, 1997], 256)

Here are several suggestions to help you define and attain success:

• **From the beginning, seek the ultimate confirmation of success.** How do you know you are successful? The key indicator is having in your heart a lasting sense of peace, harmony, and contentment; unity with loved ones; a love of life; and a sense that you are on the right pathway to eternal life. If you have that, you are successful. Some deceptive indicators are a large bank account balance, which can evaporate quickly, and worldly fame, which can fade just as fast. Inner peace comes from other sources—the noble, the charitable, the eternal.

- **Go after the kind of success that is permanent.**
To achieve lasting success, align your quest with gospel principles and ideals—family relationships, a legacy of honesty and integrity, service—contributing to lasting achievements of peace, harmony, balance, and well-being in the world. The fleeting and ephemeral are to be avoided. Aligning your success with things that are temporary, things of momentary pleasure, things that fade, will achieve nothing but darkness and emptiness. Rather, continue to strive for balance in your life. Success in business and in professional pursuits is desirable as long as priorities are aligned with the well-being and success of the family and as long as enduring principles are followed. "It is all right to own things, as long as you don't let them own you," observed John Kim. There is also such a thing as spiritual wealth, which consists of the blessings that come from following principles of enduring worth: faith, love, charity, and obedience to higher commandments. Make the attainment of that kind of wealth a central part of your life plan.
- **Make a unique and satisfying plan and follow it.**
Even with correct priorities in place and solid alignment with lasting principles, you still need a plan in order to succeed. As we reviewed earlier in this book, the essential elements of a plan are well-known: have a vision of success with realistic goals; make an action plan of things to do each day, focusing on the key actions that will leverage progress; gather all essential resources in preparation for attaining the summit; build a team of co-workers, mentors, and guides; identify the milestones along the way so as to build success one milestone at a time; and measure progress regularly, making corrections as needed—going around obstacles, over road bumps, and through adversity. No one said it would be easy—only worth it!
- **Stick with it.** Bottom line: Be sure that your desires, enthusiasm, dedication, perseverance, discipline, and

patience are adequate enough to see you through. Each of these is a subject in itself to help you succeed.

- **Desire**—This is the motivation that will keep you going.
- **Enthusiasm**—This will be contagious to all those with whom you work.
- **Dedication and perseverance**—These will ensure that you never give up. Benjamin Disraeli said, "The secret of success is constancy of purpose."
- **Discipline**—This will create an exact course for success. Cullen Hightower observed, "Failure can be bought on easy terms; success must be paid for in advance."
- **Patience**—This will keep hope alive, for time is your ally in the quest for success.

True principles applied with faith and perseverance bring success and happiness. The key is application. Periodically we need to take time to evaluate our goals and priorities to see if any dimension of our endeavor needs redirection or adjustment. Sometimes success in one area takes a person away from more important areas of life. Let's achieve a wise balance. Let's be successful at home, in the Church, in the workplace, *and* in the community.

In the King James version of the Bible, the word *success* is used only once. But this one usage is memorable, for it occurs in the passage where the Lord is counseling Moses' successor, Joshua, on how to succeed with his sacred and solemn commission to lead Israel:

> Only be thou strong and very courageous, that thou mayest observe to do according to all the law, which Moses my servant commanded thee: turn not from it to the right hand or to the left, that thou mayest prosper whithersoever thou goest. This book of the law shall not depart out of thy mouth; but thou shalt meditate therein

day and night, that thou mayest observe to do according to all that is written therein: for then thou shalt make thy way prosperous, and then thou shalt have good success. (Joshua 1:7–8)

So it is with us as well. Let us follow the word of God and triumph in the strength of the Lord. What better way is there to ensure that we will feel good, even when things seem bad?

CHAPTER TWENTY-SEVEN
COMMITTING TO GOOD WORKS AND SERVICE

Let your light so shine before men,
that they may see your good works, and glorify
your Father which is in heaven.
—Matthew 5:16

Nothing is as fulfilling as service. True service is based upon love. Serving those who cannot help themselves is a vicarious act—one of the greatest expressions of love. We lose ourselves in the service of others, and we find true power in doing so. We overcome feelings of selfishness and find joy. As we serve others, they will have a desire to serve as well, and the effect becomes not just contagious but exponential in its power to affect lives throughout the world. The feelings engendered through service bring joy that is indescribable. We will not only feel good—we'll feel lifted up and transported to a higher level of joy.

Good works and charitable service are at the heart of a covenant life. At the same time, it is not good works alone that qualify us for the blessings of heaven, which include salvation and eternal life. None of us is perfect. None can be justified by the law (as Lehi taught) without the atoning sacrifice of the Savior (see 2 Nephi 2). Beyond all of the good works and service we can perform, there must of necessity be the element of grace to carry us the remaining distance back home: "There is no flesh that can dwell in the presence of God, save it be through the merits, and mercy, and grace of the Holy Messiah, who layeth down his life according to the flesh, and taketh it again by the power of the Spirit, . . . and they that believe in him shall be saved" (2 Nephi 2:8–9).

Prophetic Counsel. President Ezra Taft Benson taught: "Reach out to others. Rather than turning inward, forget self and really serve others in your Church callings, in personal deeds of compassionate service, in unknown, unheralded personal acts of kindness" (*Come, Listen to a Prophet's Voice* [Salt Lake City: Deseret Book, 1990], 59). President Hinckley reminded us: "Those who are engaged in this service know that out of it all comes a sweet and satisfying feeling. This sweet blessing of the Spirit becomes literally a medicine to cure many of the ailments of our lives. From such experiences we come to realize that only when we serve others do we truly serve the Lord" (*Faith: The Essence of True Religion* [Salt Lake City: Deseret Book, 1989], 40).

As you continue to serve and bless the lives of others, here are several things to consider:

- **Do it with no thought of personal reward.** Unconditional service is the highest form of service. It is not a quid pro quo—it does not look for rewards or bonuses—it is done without any expectation of recognition. To make service pure, give with no thought of return. When serving, don't keep track. Service doesn't keep score. Service is timeless, and it operates on a lofty plane. Momentary pleasures are fleeting and leave no traces, whereas service is a lasting memorial to love and leaves behind an influence for good that never fades. Service is inner satisfaction, inner peace—that is reward enough.
- **Adopt the "service" habit.** The Golden Rule is the guiding principle—treating others in the same way you wish to be treated. Service and duty are partners. Some qualities of service are inherent within the family: serve with a plan (but don't forget to be spontaneous); serve proactively—taking appropriate action now rather than just saying, "Let me

know if you need any help"; serve with a willing smile; teach through example—the most enduring legacy; encourage others through a spirit of gratitude; and accept service from others with grace and appreciation.

- **Balance your service.** Service can be an expression of concern, love, or gratitude (where emotions and feelings are well served). It can be temporal as to things needed and deeds longed for. It can be intellectual if it fosters learning and growth. It can be social/emotional if it involves being a friend. It can consist of kindness to animals. It can be anything that helps or blesses everyone. You just need to follow the tracks of need—on behalf of widows, the infirm, the fatherless, the hungry, the homeless, the cold, those with special impairments, and anyone else with unfulfilled needs. You can serve your country and you can serve your God by honoring divine commandments and by loving your fellow human beings.

As we consider our lives, where we are and what we can do, let us always remember that service is multifaceted: life offers us an endless variety of ways to assist and bless others. Let us make service our life, then life will serve us well. We will have a life filled with the joy of serving. Perhaps the most succinct and memorable statement about service in the kingdom of God is this: "Pure religion and undefiled before God and the Father is this, To visit the fatherless and widows in their affliction, and to keep himself unspotted from the world" (James 1:27). In all of this, the greatest exemplar is the Savior Himself, the Father's gift to the world: "For God so loved the world, that he gave his only begotten Son, that whosoever believeth in him should not perish, but have everlasting life" (John 3:16). Let us magnify our callings and rise to the challenge of being a Zion people by giving our lives in service and good works on behalf of our families and all others within our circle of influence. When we have lives filled with the joy of serving, we will earn the blessing of feeling good—no matter what the circumstances.

Epilogue:
The Power of Prayer

Be thou diligent to know the state of thy
flocks, and look well to thy herds.
—Proverbs 27:23

When we approach our Father in Heaven asking in faith for comfort and guidance—both in good times and in bad—miracles happen. The consoling blessings of peace come from God to His children who ask with real intent, willing to accept His will, and willing to work for the righteous desires of their hearts. The old saying applies: "Pray as if everything depends upon the Lord and then work as if everything depends upon you."

President Ezra Taft Benson taught: "Our great example in prayer is our Lord and Master Jesus Christ who knew that only through constant supplication and obedience would God the Father manifest His will and release the power for its attainment through man. Truly there is power in prayer" (*The Teachings of Ezra Taft Benson* [Salt Lake City: Bookcraft, 1988], 422).

Prayer can take many forms, but the important thing is for our prayers to be sincere and genuine. Prayer partakes of many elements—especially vision, love, gratitude, humility, faith, and patience. Prayer's effectiveness can be magnified in many ways—by our praying often, seeking confirmation of our best-thought-out solutions, focusing on the needs of others, and acting always from a broken heart and contrite spirit. Prayer and wisdom go hand in hand in many ways when we pray for the right kinds of things, such as strength to overcome our challenges, understanding to magnify our callings, forgiveness of our wrong-doings, and guidance in blessing our families. If we fill our lives with prayer and devotion, we will find that blessings and knowledge will flow to us "as the dews from heaven" (D&C 121:45).

The Savior taught: "Ask, and it shall be given unto you; seek, and ye shall find; knock, and it shall be opened unto you" (3 Nephi 14:7; compare Matthew 7:7). When we pray, our lives will be enriched. We will have greater power to do good. Life will be more meaningful, fulfilling, and enjoyable. And we will feel good, whether in times of abundance or scarcity, succor or want, health or sickness—for with the Lord's help, we can do all things and stay forever on the bright side.

APPENDIX

Things to Do and Questions to Ask Yourself When You Want to Feel Good:

- Smile.
- Laugh a little more.
- Choose to change.
- Make up a righteous reason for someone's apparent misdeed.
- Forgive immediately.
- Practice patience.
- Look to the solution—don't blame others.
- Is this important?
- Will it matter tomorrow or next year?
- What really matters?
- Is this a simple mistake?
- Don't dwell on simple mistakes or mishaps.
- Does this require action or a response?
- If something requires action—do it; don't procrastinate.
- Does this affect someone's eternal life?
- What are the real damages?
- Be understanding and helpful.
- Rejoice over the birth of a child.
- Do a deed of sacrifice for a child.
- Finish homework early.
- Practice a skill or talent.
- Lift weights and exercise.
- Do training for something special.
- Keep the commandments.

- Remember that work takes time and effort and can be hard—but it's worth it.
- Have a positive attitude.
- Have a true perception of life.
- Do random acts of kindness.
- Always ask, "What would Jesus do?"
- Spend time with those you love.
- Volunteer your services to others and to good causes.
- Serve those who can't serve themselves.
- Count your blessings.
- Remember the less fortunate and needy.
- Sing a song.
- Hum a tune.
- Stay on your diet—at least one more day.
- Compliment someone.
- Buy a little present for someone.
- Treat yourself with a moment of free time or a little present.
- Act well the part and you'll become what you want to become.
- Don't be obsessed with perfection—just do your best.
- Be flexible.
- Eat well.
- Remember the good times and write them in your journal.
- Write a letter of gratitude to someone.
- Call someone on the phone and praise them for the good they have done.
- Take a hot shower.
- Have a bubble bath.
- Sit down and read a good book.
- Call a close friend or relative and tell them you love them.
- Imagine yourself in your favorite place.
- When you wake up early, just lie in bed and think you don't have to get up—yet.

- Pet a dog (a friendly one).
- Let a child win a race or a game.
- Go for a little walk.
- When you wake up tomorrow, think about how grateful you are that you can get up.
- Go to a website that has some good clean laughs.
- Play music you enjoyed as a youth—and see if it is still really good.
- Spend time doing your favorite things, including your hobbies.
- Think of something fun to do on a bad weather day.
- Write down your plans for the day, and when they are accomplished, cross them off.
- Control your thoughts—thoughts can really matter.
- Think how this applies to you: "For as he thinketh in his heart, so is he" (Proverbs 23:7).
- Ponder: How can thoughts have such a powerful effect upon behavior? Does the mind really control matter—even our attitude and behavior? (The answer is a resounding, "Yes"!)

Where will your thoughts take you today? Thoughts, dwelt upon, become desires, which, when encouraged, result in action. You do what you think. So think good thoughts.

TOPICAL INDEX